Philosophers and Religious Truth

NINIAN SMART

Philosophers and Religious Truth

SCM PRESS LTD

For Roderick

334   01258 9

First published 1964
by SCM Press Ltd
56 Bloomsbury Street London WC1
Second edition 1969

© SCM Press Ltd 1964, 1969

Printed in Great Britain by
Northumberland Press Ltd
Gateshead

CONTENTS

PREFACE

The aim of this book is to exhibit the philosophy of religion in action. Naturally, I have mainly concentrated on issues which have been much discussed by philosophers. As evidence of this, I have made each chapter, except the first, grow from the views of some past philosopher. In some degree, therefore, I have neglected a lot of the contemporary *theological* debate. This may prove an advantage, even for those with theological inclinations. In so far as the leading theologians of our day have been philosophical, they have tended to be Existentialist. Existentialism has its insights, but it is often opaque and anti-intellectual. There are merits, then, in a more commonsensical and (I hope) clear discussion of important religious issues. Most agnostics whom I know reject religion on philosophical grounds, that is on general intellectual ones; and the appeals to revelation or to personal commitment, which figure so much in Existentialist theology, cut little ice. It does not take much acumen to see that the world has many religions (so why choose Christianity?) and that decisions presuppose a view of the truth (so why conjure up God out of mere commitment?). Nor is it the case that my agnostic friends are all 'educated' folk. They talk about science, a new God and not an unreasonable one. They express, often in an unsophisticated way, the chief issue in the philosophy of religion.

Anyway, the divisions between theology, philosophy and science are rather artificial. Modern Protestant theology tends to neglect the literal story of the Fall: modern biology is responsible for this situation. Yet many Christians go on saying the same old things, and meaning them differently—for is it not said 'Science deals with the one aspect of reality, faith with another'? But such a complete cease-fire between the two realms, with some philosophers acting as UNO, settles nothing. Nor does it help to be told that 'religionless Christianity' is the thing—even by a Bonhoeffer (martyrdom is not the only qualification for true thinking); and it helps little to be told that 'deep down' rather than 'out there' is the spatial metaphor which OK people should use.

So there remain many incisive questions about the idea of God. I do not at all pretend to answer many or any. But it is worth thinking in a reasonably hard-headed way about some of these issues. I hope my discussion will be of some use, if only as a stimulant to answers other than mine. In this area, paradoxically, dogmatism and text-book solutions are useless.

It will be noticed that I have numbered the paragraphs throughout the book. This serves two functions. First, it enables me to make easy cross-references: and if the reader forgets what has gone before, these help. Second, I include at the end a list of books and articles, arranged by reference to the relevant paragraphs. Thus the reader can pursue particular topics in more detail, if he wishes.

The SCM Press through the Rev. David Edwards and Professors Ian Ramsey and John McIntyre, have been helpfully critical of my effort: the Editor has also been patient of delays. Mrs Papps, Mrs Miller, Mrs Strachan, and Miss Toy have been chiefly and happily instrumental in typing my manuscript. I thank all these.

NINIAN SMART

PREFACE TO SECOND EDITION

At the suggestion of the Rev. John Bowden, Editor of the SCM Press, I have added a further chapter to the original. It is perhaps less closely integrated with the rest of the argument than the other chapters, but follows on naturally, since it deals with questions about a future life, left largely on one side in the earlier discussions, but an obvious lacuna in those discussions. This lacuna was mentioned in my original postscript. I have substituted a new postscript, together with a brief biographical paragraph about Wittgenstein on p. 12. Apart from these additions, etc., the rest of the book is unaltered, save for the correction of one or two misprints.

February 1969   N. S.

THE SIX MEN STUDIED IN THIS BOOK

DAVID HUME 1711-76

Born and died in Edinburgh. His *Essay on Miracles* was published in 1748, and his *Dialogues concerning Natural Religion* after his death. Today he is regarded as the greatest of British philosophers, and his critical attitude towards traditional religion has been influential. See A. H. Basson, *David Hume* (Pelican Book); *Hume on Religion* (Fontana Book).

IMMANUEL KANT 1724-1804

Born in Königsberg, East Prussia, he became Professor of Logic and Metaphysics at the university there. His *Critique of Pure Reason* and *Critique of Practical Reason* are classics of philosophy. See S. Körner, *Kant* (Pelican Book).

ST THOMAS AQUINAS 1224-74

An Italian who taught philosophy at Paris and elsewhere. The greatest thinker of the Middle Ages, in his *Summa Theologica* and *Summa contra Gentiles* he bequeathed a massive intellectual system, reconciling the philosophy of Aristotle with the Catholic faith. See F. C. Copleston, *Aquinas* (Pelican Book).

RUDOLF OTTO 1869-1937

In 1917 he became a Professor at Marburg University in Germany and published his most famous book, *The Idea of the Holy* (now a Pelican Book). A student of Eastern religions, he stressed the universality of religious experience.

F. R. TENNANT 1866-1957

He studied science at Cambridge, served as an Anglican chaplain, and became University Lecturer in the Philosophy of Religion in 1913. The two volumes of his *Philosophical Theology* were published in 1928-30. These volumes, with other books on miracles and on sin, presented a calmly rational belief in God.

LUDWIG WITTGENSTEIN 1889-1951

Born in Vienna, he studied engineering, but became increasingly interested in logic and philosophy. He came to Cambridge in 1912 to work with Russell. His *Tractatus Logico-Philosophicus* was published in German in 1918 and in German and English in 1922. He gave up philosophy for a time, but returned to Cambridge in 1930, eventually succeeding G. E. Moore in his chair. The main fruit of his later period was the posthumous *Philosophical Investigations*.

I

Philosophers and Religious Truth

1.1 L I F E is both strange and commonplace. But for most of the time it is commonplace, and we are not surprised that the world is as it is, for we have no experience of any other modes of existence. The surprises that come our way are only surprises within an un-surprising framework. It may astonish us that Henry has suddenly entered a monastery or that the government of France has been overthrown, but Henry and monasteries and governments and France are part of the order of things. Yet every so often the whole set-up may suddenly strike us as strange. We find ourselves in a universe containing, among other things, France and monasteries: but why should there be a universe at all? Why should it contain conscious, rational beings like ourselves? And what is the world really like? Are the things we see around us really as they seem to be – bathed in colour and light and shade? Or is this only an appearance that our brains and minds foist upon them? Such questions arise from, and themselves also supply, the sense of strangeness that can sometimes afflict us. The universe is our home; and yet now and then we look around uneasily, wondering whether all the time it is a stranger's house. Out of this unease and strange-ness and wonder, science and philosophy spring. Men who feel this strangeness are no longer immersed in the flow of life: they are beginning to contemplate it and to try to understand its secrets.

1.2 In the new light of such contemplation, everything comes under scrutiny. We may, for instance, have been brought up to worship God, to be pious in our religious duties. Even this solemn and central feature of life is, to the person who does not reflect, and who remains immersed in the flow of existence, commonplace. That God reveals himself to men, that some men respond to this and go to church, that you shut your eyes when you pray – these facts seem quite normal. This is how things are. But as soon as the philosophical sense of strangeness begins to afflict us, all these commonplaces take on a new and uncanny look. Philosophy brings religion under scrutiny, just as it questions the other facets of life and of existence.

1.3 In relation to religious truth, philosophy is ambiguous. It is at once a menace and an ally. It is a menace, because the sense of wonder issues in the question 'Why should things be so?' More particularly, why should revelation or ecclesiastical authority be accepted? How can anyone claim to know the mysteries of God? Perhaps the pretensions of faith all rest upon illusion. In such ways, philosophy is menacing to revelation and piety. For as soon as we ask questions of this kind, simple faith, and sometimes even sophisticated faith, is seen to be inadequate. Of course, it would be silly to suppose that therefore simple folk cannot be good Christians, or that you have to be something of a philosopher to have spiritual respectability. Still, if you become aware of these questions, if they bite into you so that you cannot shake yourself free from them, then it is no use trying to hide from this particular form of your destiny and to take refuge in simple faith. Unfortunately there are many who in effect have done just this. Profoundly disturbed by the questions, and by the unnerving impact of modern science upon traditional beliefs, they throw away their intellects. They cling to the literal inerrancy of scripture or to some other clearcut authority, and build a wall in their minds to keep out science and philosophy from the domain of faith. One can well understand this: and indeed one can sympathize with their predicament. But it is not a happy destiny, nor is it a fully human one. The universe must be faced, and the truth about reality cannot in this simple way be prejudged. So if the philosophical fate is your fate, then it is as well to be clear that it is, as far as faith goes, a menacing one. But, as I said, philosophy is ambiguous. The questioning attitude of mind can, paradoxically, also be an ally of the religious spirit.

1.4 If God is just a commonplace, religious devotion and understanding can be merely superficial. Perhaps this is why saintliness and doubts often go together. A God who is accepted simply as an unsurprising part of reality, and as a Person who quite as a matter of course supplies a revelation, has no real majesty, mystery or depth. He is anthropomorphic – an invisible man writ large. But if the world strikes us in all its strangeness, then suddenly religion acquires a new significance. It really is most odd, how men bow down and worship, how they perform bizarre rituals. It seems like a kind of madness to talk of God, to search for the unseen. The madness, though, may be the madness of genius, and the invisible reality may have an uncanny glory, once we penetrate beyond the commonplace attitudes of piety. The philosophical spirit, by liberating us from a humdrum view of life, may bring depth to our understanding of faith. In such a way, for all its menace, it can be an ally.

1.5 But it would not be philosophical to predict in advance how things will turn out in the pursuit of truth. Of course, there is room for hunches: maybe we feel at the outset that truth must be like this or that. Nevertheless, once we are committed by our intellectual destiny to asking certain sorts of questions, to asking the uncomfortable questions about the truth of religion, then it would be wrong to tame the menace by laying it down that in the end everything will be all right.

1.6 It may be noted that I have not tried to define philosophy, though I have used the word several times. One reason is that, owing to the peculiar and changing nature of philosophical enquiry, a neat verbal definition would be both inadequate and misleading. It is better to understand what philosophy is by doing some philosophy, just as we learn what music is by listening to it and by playing it. It is the process of thinking that is important, the process of question and answer and discussion. I shall therefore say no more about the aims of this book than this: that I hope in the course of it to indulge in such a process and to show what issues are important for the person who thinks about religion. Thus we may arrive at some solutions of the problems that are posed. I do not say that these are the only solutions: for, as will become apparent, philosophical argument is rarely knock-down and definitive. And though my conclusions (it is best to come clean about this at the outset) are fairly favourable to Christian faith, I have no doubt that the progress of science, and the probings of philosophers, have rendered it less easy to adhere to traditional formulations of faith. Nevertheless, I hope that in fact my arguments contain truth, and that, even despite the altered intellectual climate, it is reasonable to believe in the truth of Christianity.

1.7 Reasonable? But some may jib at the word. It suggests that one has to be judicious and cautiously rational about religion. But how does this square with the need for faith and commitment? Faith does not wait upon philosophy or seek powerful reasonings in its support. It is a response to Christ, and there is something gloriously *un*reasonable about this. No wonder there has sometimes been, in the history of Christianity, great conflict between theologians and philosophers.

1.8 But let us be clear about the issues at stake. It is necessary to distinguish between the truth and commitment. What is the case or what is not the case does not depend upon what men do, or upon their commitments. Of course, it may be that we cannot *apprehend* certain truths unless we are somehow committed. It may turn out, therefore, that unless I am committed to a person, for instance, a friend or wife, that I shall not understand his or her feelings, that an 'objective' and uncommitted approach to a person will rule out any genuine knowledge of his heart and mind. Nevertheless, it would be bizarre to suggest that the nature of reality, or the nature of God, *depended* upon our responses. God does not *become* the Creator of the universe in virtue of our commitment to him. This would indeed be blasphemy, to think that we had him that much in our power. But, now, if we so distinguish between truth and commitment, it is never enough that we should be committed. For instance, the sincere and energetic Marxist is no doubt considerably committed. But is Marxism true? If it is false, or in its political and moral directives wrong-headed, what profit is it that Marxists are committed? Well, it makes us admire them more as persons; for sincerity, though it makes wrong-headed people more dangerous, deserves respect. But what is true and good is vitally important too.

1.9 What, then, is the quarrel with the idea that faith should be reasonable? If we hold that something is true, do we not have to have reasons for holding that it is true? If I trust someone, do I not have reasons for trusting him? Every time I step on a bus, I am displaying a certain faith – I have faith in the driver: I believe that he will not be rash and negligent in his driving. And why? Well, I know that drivers are properly trained, that disciplinary action would be taken against a man who kept swigging brandy as he drove up Oxford Street, that most people are reasonably responsible anyway, that dangerous driving brings as much risk to the driver as to the passengers. Of course, I might be unlucky: but still, I have good reasons for committing myself to the driver's care.

1.10 Nevertheless, this example is of a puny commitment, and one which comes well within the bounds of prudence. Isn't that the point of saying that commitment to Christ is unreasonable rather than it is imprudent? For we often use the word 'reasonable' in the following way: we talk of what is reasonable or unreasonable to demand of someone, as though moderation must be used in asking favours; for we cannot normally expect a man to sacrifice his deeper interests, and to be imprudent on behalf of others. It is perhaps in this sense that commitment to Christ is unreasonable, since it may mean that sacrificial demands are made upon the faithful. But this has little to do with the question of whether we have good reasons or grounds for believing the doctrines of Christianity. Christianity may be reasonable, in *this* sense, and yet make 'unreasonable' demands.

1.11 No, it is in rather a different context, namely the context of truth, that there is liable to be a conflict between philosophy and theology. Historically, philosophers have not just been content with asking the sceptical questions which arise out of the sense of strangeness that the world sometimes presents: but they have gone on to try to depict the inner nature of reality, and to give a comprehensive account of the world – an endeavour usually called 'metaphysics'.

Thus for instance Plato attempted to delineate, through his theory of Forms, the relation between this world and the transcendent, invisible world which somehow lay behind or beyond it. The comprehensiveness, subtlety and high moral tone of his teachings were bound to impress the early Church. But there remained the danger that in attempting to adapt and use Plato's metaphysical system Christian thinkers would alter and betray the essential insights of revelation. The God thought out by the philosopher and the God who revealed himself to the prophets are not necessarily compatible. Hence there has been a recurring feeling among Christians that the divine revelation has been obscured by its contact with Greek philosophy; and that later systems of thought have likewise tended to replace the living God with abstractions made by men. If revelation comes from God, and if faith comes through the grace of God, how can men pretend, through their own efforts and through the exercise of their own powers of reasoning, to arrive at a knowledge of God? In the last century, the Danish writer Kierkegaard, who has had such a profound effect upon Christian thinking, and who also may be reckoned the forerunner of Existentialism, entered a violent protest against the whole system of Hegel who had tried to show that reality was a single spiritual whole, or Absolute. Kierkegaard felt that Hegel's use of reason not only left no real place for faith, but also wrongly substituted an abstract Absolute for a personal God who takes the initiative in revealing himself to men. And so, in the history of Christian thought, there has been an ambiguous response to metaphysics. Christians have been grateful that there should be some positive attempt to delineate the nature of reality independently of revelation; but they have also been unhappy that often such an attempt issues in conclusions which obscure the truths of revelation. Thus both the sceptical philosopher, like Hume, who undermines the basis of religious belief, and the metaphysical philosopher, like Hegel, who provides a basis for such belief but only when it is made to conform to philosophical ideas – both kinds of philosopher may be in conflict with theology.

1.12 This situation leads to paradoxical results. For sometimes Christians have stressed the need for natural theology, i.e. for a knowledge of God which does not depend upon revelation; and at other times, they have welcomed scepticism, since the destruction of any kind of rational knowledge of ultimate reality seems to leave room for faith. Thus, on the one hand, St Thomas Aquinas, by adapting and transforming the thought of Aristotle, constructed a system of natural theology which has for seven centuries dominated Roman Catholic philosophy. On the other hand, Dean Mansel, in his famous Bampton Lectures delivered in 1858, argued that all views of ultimate reality involve contradictions, and that we could know nothing about it. All we can do is to label it an 'unknown X'. But, mysteriously, and beyond the grasp of human reasoning, this unknown X reveals itself personally to men, through Christ. Thus for Mansel, as for Kierkegaard, the destruction of pretentious reason leaves room for faith. At the present time, under the influence of Logical Positivism and of its succeeding lines of thought, some philosophers, in defending Christianity, have similarly attempted to count the death of metaphysics a blessing, for out of it faith can be born. But the situation is nevertheless ironical. If philosophers say 'God's existence can be proved', Christians will smile with contentment. But if philosophers say 'God's existence is unprovable', Christians may likewise smile with contentment. Whatever happens, it is all right. It is as though the Christian were saying: 'There are two good grounds for Christian faith – first, that God's existence can be demonstrated rationally, and second that there is no hope whatsoever of demonstrating God's existence rationally.'

1.13 This ironic state of affairs may induce a feeling of despair about philosophy. If faith is going to survive anyway, whatever reasoning has to say, then why bother with reasoning? But such despair is mistaken. As we have already seen, the questions which an intelligent man raises about the truth of religion are unavoidable. Moreover, in what sense does faith survive anyway? It is an obvious feature of Western society that a large number of intelligent people are agnostics. This is not just perversity on their part, or due simply to moral defects (though some Christians might find such a hypothesis most attractive). It is because they find Christianity unpersuasive, incredible. It is not that they do not *want* to believe it: it is just that they *cannot* believe it. And this impossibility of belief, for such persons, springs from their estimate of the evidence. Now no doubt we may reply that their estimate is mistaken, that the evidences and grounds of belief are stronger than they think, that if the matter were approached in the right way they would see the light. All this may be so. But it implies that there are evidences, that there are grounds, that there is a right way of approach. Faith is not a blind leap in the dark. But this means that Christian apologetics is vitally important. If ever Christians were to find that they could muster no plausible historical evidence, that there was no ground for faith, that only by totally abandoning the use of reason could you believe the Creeds, then faith would have a strange kind of survival. It would survive among the ill-educated, among those who were not 'whole men' and who built a wall in their minds (1.3), among the unbalanced. Christianity would become like the faith of Jehovah's Witnesses: and a good education (one which led to the capacity for genuine reflection about fundamental issues) would be an effective bar to heaven. If Christianity involved such a deep and radical affront to the whole modern scientific world-picture, then belief in it would be on a par with those curious lunacies which mysteriously still survive in an educated nation – belief, for instance, that the earth is flat, or that we are really 'insiders', living on the inside, not the outside, of a spherical earth. Faith, then, might survive (no doubt ecclesiastical organization would see to that), but it would have paid a bitter and intolerable price.

1.14 Thus, though there is irony in the fact that opposite philosophical conclusions are sometimes hailed as allies of faith, the enterprise of philosophizing about the faith cannot be escaped. Christians believe in Christian doctrines because they believe that they are true. This indeed should be a tautology. But truth demands evidence. We cannot *decide* that something is true the way we can decide to play patience.

1.15 But, anyway, the situation is less ironical than at first appears, and for two reasons. First, both philosophical and religious arguments are rarely, if ever, of a clear-cut and decisive nature. This is partly because in both spheres the criteria of truth (the tests of whether a statement is true) are difficult to settle in advance. If we are asked whether there are any elephants in Ethiopia, we know how to set about answering; for we know where the country is, and we know what counts as an elephant. All this we know as soon as the question is asked. But if we are asked whether something is an experience of God, it is not so easy. What counts as such an experience? What is the nature of God? About both these questions there is a lot of room for disagreement. No doubt this unclarity about criteria is in the nature of the case. God is not to be found, like an elephant, in time and space, nor is he something which can be neatly observed and labelled. It is not therefore surprising that differing theories and philosophical doctrines should be held by religious people. The second reason why the situation is not so ironical as at first appears is that both the metaphysical defender of the faith, like Aquinas, and the sceptical defender of the faith, like Kierkegaard, display profound insights into religious truth. It may be after all that from each you can extract something of value. For instance, the line of thought initiated by Kierkegaard has led theologians to see that revelation involves a personal and existential encounter between God and man, and is not simply to be regarded as a string of propositions infallibly uttered by God. On the other hand, Kierkegaard's protest against metaphysics is really a protest against Hegel. If Hegel is false, this does not mean that *all reasonings* about God are false. Thus, there may still be something of importance in Aquinas' claim that there are some truths about God which can be seen to be true independently of revelation. It is not at all absurd to hold that this *must* be so. For if God be creator of the universe, we must have some reason for holding that the God who is met with in the encounter of faith is indeed the Creator. I may have experience of a personal Being; but does the experience *in itself* show that this Being created the atoms which I tread underfoot? Obviously, those arguments which attempt to show that the cosmos must be dependent on some Being outside it are highly relevant to this issue. Furthermore, it is clear that in regard to religious truth it is insufficient simply to appeal to revelation, whether this be conceived as propositions or as encounter: for in the world there are different sacred books, and men of varying religions have claimed a personal awareness of ultimate reality. How are we to know which claims are true, and how they are to be interpreted? To know these things we must in some sense go beyond our own books and our own encounters.

1.16 It will already be seen that commitment to the philosophical enterprise of scrutinizing the nature and grounds of religious truth will take us far afield. In one direction, it takes us into scientific enquiry – since, for instance, any discussion of the Creation needs to take account of modern theories in cosmology. Further, it may well be asked whether the appeal to revelation is compatible with the spirit of science. The Christian claims to know something about ultimate reality on a basis other than that of observation and experiment, and yet these constitute the main tests of truth in science. But not merely does the enquiry take us into science: it also takes us into neighbouring philosophical fields. For instance, the Christian faith has a strong historical root, and would be nothing without the events of Christ's life, death and resurrection. But if Christ rose truly from the dead, this is indeed a miracle – apparently an infringement of the laws of nature. Yet some philosophers have said that no rational person could believe in miracles, or that there is something incoherent in the idea that calling an event a miracle can explain anything. Again, the capacity of men to respond to God's revelation, and in particular to his commands, is often taken to imply that men have free will. But this again appears to infringe laws of nature – for are not all events determined by laws? If what I am going to do is already fixed by my constitution and environment, how can I be said to be *free*? Not only does philosophy involve us in these traditional questions, but it leads us still further. For the capacity to respond to God sometimes, so it is said, yields intimate experience of God. What of St Paul, and what of the great mystics of the Christian Church? Indeed, many Christians derive their certainty that Christ is Lord from inner experience. And yet we are here presented with the challenge of other faiths and of other traditions and cultures. The Hindu and the Buddhist likewise claim that they can attain a mystical experience, or that a divine Lord appears to them. If they too look to experience, why should we say that Christianity is true and yet Hinduism and Buddhism are not? It would seem that the philosopher must have some acquaintance not only with science, when he moves in one direction, but

also with the great religions, when he moves in another. The area
of his vision must indeed be vast. It is perhaps difficult or impossible
for anyone to be competent to judge such a variety of questions.
But the job has to be done; and since it is such an important one it
is better that it be undertaken inadequately than that it should be
left aside altogether. In the following chapters I hope, then, to
indicate what the range of problems confronting us is, and to try to
work out some solutions.

1.17 But it is hard to know where to start. It would be traditional
to begin with an examination of the proofs which have been offered
for the existence of God, but it is perhaps preferable to come to
these later. For one thing, faith does not usually start from there.
We do not come to faith through a metaphysical enquiry – and
though, as I have said (1.13), such an enquiry seems to me indispensable, it is more realistic to start with revelation, for when
philosophers attempt to prove God's existence they do not do so in
a vacuum: always at the back of their minds is a richer conception
of God than that which is arrived at in the process of philosophical
argument. That richer conception, of course, is derived from revelation. Another reason why it is better to start elsewhere than with
the traditional proofs of God's existence is that I hope to use some
of the ideas incorporated in my attempts to solve other problems
in discussing these proofs.

1.18 But from what aspect of revelation should we start? Again,
to be realistic, if we are thinking of European religious thought,
the life, death and resurrection of Christ must be seen as central.
But of course it is not for the philosopher to take the place of the
theologian and preacher and to attempt on his own account
an exposition of Christ's teachings or of the significance of the
Cross. Rather his job is to examine the way in which the typical
and central Christian affirmations fit in with beliefs which we hold
in other connections – with scientific thinking, for example; and by
consequence likewise his job is to see how the truth of religion can
be established. In both these connections, the problem of miracles
is clearly important – for on the one hand belief in miracles seems
at first sight to run counter to the scientific desire to banish the in-

explicable; and on the other hand the truth of Christianity seems to be very much bound up with the truth of the stories of the resurrection of Christ. Therefore I shall start with the problem of miracles; and this will serve too to introduce the powerful arguments brought to bear on the problem by David Hume. Though he lived two centuries ago, his influence remains strong in modern philosophy; and many intellectuals, philosophers and otherwise, remain sympathetic to the urbane religious scepticism which he expressed. Also, though the problem of miracles is somewhat neglected in the contemporary discussion of religion, it happens that (as I have indicated above) the issues raised in the next chapter form the starting-point for the treatment of other important themes. In this way, the rest of the book is intended as, in effect, a single continuous argument.

2

Miracles and David Hume

2.1 CHRISTIAN belief means accepting the resurrection of Christ, and therefore it seems to involve believing in at least one miracle. There are other miracles, of course, recorded in the Gospels, and perhaps about some of these we may feel doubts – doubts as to whether the writers of the Gospels have accurately recorded the facts, or again doubts as to whether some of the supposed miracles are really miraculous. The healing miracles, for instance, might be accounted for by saying that the cures may be psychosomatic in origin. But if there is an irreducible core of the miraculous in Christian belief, then that belief must inevitably face up to the philosophical and other problems which cluster round the concept.

2.2 It is true that Christians today feel much less inclined than were their predecessors in the eighteenth century to see in miracles a kind of guarantee of the authenticity of revelation. Christ (so it was fashionable to think) showed, in turning water into wine, in raising the dead, in healing the blind, that he brought God's message. This view of the miraculous suggested that these strange events were a kind of hall-mark placed upon his claims to show that they were authentic. Nowadays we feel somewhat uneasy about this rather simple view of miracles and of the way in which a genuine revelation is validated. For one thing, there is an increasing awareness of the danger (remarked upon by Christ himself) of treating miracles as external signs, having nothing else to do with Christ's mission than to show its authenticity. To be a 'proof' of Christ's divinity a miracle could take any form: and if the function of the miracles was to provide powerful evidence of his authenticity, why should he not have performed something much more spectacular? Moreover, if revelation is not just a matter of claims, teachings, propositions (1.15), but is properly speaking the self-disclosure of God, then anything miraculous done by Christ must be an integral part of that self-disclosure, and not an external guarantee of truth. For these reasons, we can see that it is crude and naïve to think of miracles as guaranteeing the truth of scriptures.

2.3 But nevertheless, as has been said, one cannot have Christian belief without accepting at least some miraculous element in Christ's life. It is therefore disturbing to discover the powerful argument, in his *Essay on Miracles*, produced by Hume against such belief. Briefly it was this.

2.4 A wise man proportions his belief to the evidence. If experience shows without exception that a certain type of event occurs (e.g. that water freezes at a certain temperature), then he has proof that this will happen in the future. In other cases, his judgment is based on *probability*. Thus if he has found more instances of the occurrence of an event in certain conditions than of its non-occurrence, he concludes that it is probable that the event will occur on a particular occasion in the future. He balances the pros against the cons. Similar remarks apply when he takes into account the testimony of other humans. He has found by experience that humans on the whole tell the truth, can remember events and so on. If he is told something extraordinary, he has to weigh the pros (the usual reliability of testimony) against the cons (what he has observed in his own experience and what he has been told about the normal observations of others). In the weighing of them, he arrives at a verdict.

2.5 Now a miracle, properly so-called, is not something which is merely extraordinary: it is something which violates a law of nature. For instance, it is a law of nature that people do not physically rise from the dead: for observation uniformly shows that after certain events which we call 'death' (the stopping of the heart, the ceasing to function of the brain, etc.) physical dissolution sets in, so that the body cannot be active any more. It is a law of nature that water freezes at a certain temperature. How do we know that these are laws of nature? On the basis of experience, of unfailing observation. If we always see that such-and-such happens, we conclude that such-and-such always happens. Now it is not enough that a miracle should be something extraordinary, like an earthquake in Wigan, for we could think up an ordinary explanation for that sort of thing. Thus a miracle has to be something like a man rising from the dead, really recovering physically from real death.

2.6 It follows, argues Hume, that it could never be reasonable to believe in a miracle. For against the testimony of human beings (the pros) there is our universal experience of the law of nature (the cons). The cons must have it. For it is surely more credible that humans have been deceived or themselves deceive than that something contrary to our whole previous experience of the world should occur. Even if we had testimony amounting to proof, we have proof the other way too: and so we would have to choose between the two miracles – the miracle of a resurrection and the miracle of a mistake after all in the testimony. When in doubt, choose the lesser miracle; and the second miracle is the lesser.

2.7 But of course, says Hume, in any case testimony in these matters never amounts to proof. First, we have not, in all history, any miracle attested by men of such good sense, education and learning as to secure us against delusion. Second, men like the emotions of surprise and wonder, and these are catered for by tales of the miraculous. Third, miracles chiefly abound among uncivilized peoples, and those civilized nations that accept them have generally been found to derive them from ignorant ancestors. Fourth, different religions appeal to miracles as establishing their truth. In so doing they discredit the miracles of other faiths, and thereby discredit their own miracles. Thus we have reasons, based upon historical experience, for being suspicious of accounts of miracles, and we never have anything amounting to proof of them. Hence, in the conflict between universal experience and testimony on behalf of a miracle, it is never reasonable to accept the latter and to reject the former.

2.8   Hume concludes his *Essay on Miracles* ironically: 'The Christ- ian religion not only was at first attended with miracles, but even at this day cannot be believed by any reasonable person without one. Mere reason is insufficient to convince us of its veracity: and whoever is moved by faith to assent to it is conscious of a continued miracle in his own person, which subverts all the principles of his understanding, and gives him a determination to believe what is most contrary to custom and experience.'

2.9   Such is Hume's argument, and it appears powerful. But it has one or two paradoxical consequences. These we shall come to; but first let us glance at what Hume says elsewhere about the idea of a cause, for a miracle, by running contrary to a law of nature, may appear to be uncaused, or rather it is not physically caused, though supposedly caused by God, supernaturally. What he says elsewhere at first seems to contradict the notion that universal experience of a phenomenon amounts to proof that it will occur in the future. For Hume is at pains to argue that there is no *necessity* in causation. Though we have the idea that when an event causes another there is a necessary connexion between the two, as though the occurrence of the one in some way makes it necessary that the other should occur, this idea cannot be given a basis in experience. From the empirical point of view, i.e. resting our argument solely on experi- ence, all we are entitled to say is that whenever an event of type A occurs, we find that an event of type B occurs. There is a constant conjunction between the two; but we cannot observe anything over and above this which we can call a necessity. As we shall see, this view of Hume's had consequences about the nature of science which were important, and which roused Kant from what he called his 'dogmatic slumber', impelling him to think out afresh the basis of scientific explanation.

2.10   Hume's point about necessity may be seen in a different light by considering what it means about the future. If the connexion of causes and effects simply amounts to regular succession, then there is no necessity that this regular succession should continue in the future. The sun rises daily, with cheerful regularity. But how do we know that it will do so tomorrow? That there has been a regular sequence in the past does not imply necessarily that the sun will go on being regular. Indeed, there is no contradiction between saying

(1) The sun has always risen in the past; and
(2) The sun will not rise tomorrow.

This point of course applies not merely to the sun but to all regularities whatsoever, to all laws of nature, to all casual sequences. And this generates what philosophers have called 'the problem of induction'. Induction is when we arrive at conclusions on the basis of experience; as opposed to deduction, as in mathematics, where we work out conclusions without direct reference to experience. The problem is this:

2.11 Science discovers laws of nature, e.g. that water freezes at a certain temperature. But these laws refer both to past and future: what kind of a science is it if it says that water freezes at such-and-such a temperature, but not tomorrow! But the reference to the future is only valid upon the assumption that nature is uniform, that what has been will be. The uniformity of nature can only, however, be established upon the basis of observation. But observation is past observation and present observation, not future observation. I can't directly observe what will go on tomorrow. Consequently, we can only establish the uniformity of nature upon the assumption that what has been will be. But this is the very assumption of the uniformity of nature which we are trying to establish. The attempt to establish it is circular. Ergo, it cannot be established. The consequence is that science seems to rest upon an unprovable assumption. And this is seemingly a rather embarrassing situation.

2.12 It is one which was clarified by Hume. The point is immediately relevant to the discussion on miracles. For if it is not contradictory to suppose that water might not freeze in the same way tomorrow, it cannot be contradictory to suppose that an event occurs which 'violates a law of nature'. The miraculous is not self-contradictory. At most it is incredible, and it is the latter which Hume is setting out to show.

2.13 But if it is not self-contradictory to say that the sun won't rise tomorrow, how can we claim, on the basis of experience, to have a *proof* that it won't? Certainly, if we are thinking of mathematics as a model, we cannot say that we have a proof. For in logic and mathematics a proof is precisely this: showing that the conclusion cannot fail to follow. It would be a self-contradiction if the conclusion did not follow. But if our propositions (1) and (2) above (2.10) do not contradict each other, how can (1) be taken as proving the contradictory of (2)? How can the past rising of the sun show that its future non-rising is impossible?

2.14 But it may well be misguided to think of all proof as though it must be of the mathematical type. The detective who proves that the murderer was Smithson can produce a clinching argument. But we would be surprised if he set it out like Euclid: it isn't after all meant to be a mathematical deduction. If I say that I can prove to you that I can ride a wild pony, I won't get out paper and ink, but rather will produce clinching evidence by riding the beast. When a Scottish jury brings in a verdict of not proven, it is not because the prosecution have failed in deduction, but because the evidence fails to clinch the matter. Certainly, in ordinary language we recognize that the word 'proof' applies differently in different areas. And the attempt to make empirical enquiries, such as science, conform to a mathematical model may be quite misguided. It may be like saying 'Jones is a poor footballer, for he never hits a boundary'. This involves judging him by an inappropriate standard. One can gain certainty of the mathematical sort only by making truths true by definition, but in so doing one shrivels up their empirical consequences. 'All bachelors are unmarried' is a happily certain truth; but I know it without examining young men. It is about words, or rather it springs from the use of words; but it tells us nothing about observable reality. Whatever the real world was like it would remain true, for 'unmarried' is part of the meaning of 'bachelor' – whereas 'All bachelors are melancholy' would not. To be about reality, a truth has to take the risk of being false.

2.15 But even if in spite of this we still feel that it is sad that empirical science can never have the certainty of mathematical deduction, we should still be reasonable and seek only that degree of certainty which is possible. And whatever the ultimate philosophical implications are of the fact that error and illusion are always theoretically possible, however sure an empirical conclusion may be, we can nevertheless recognize that in certain cases we can achieve the best proof which is possible in the empirical realm.

2.16 We should not say that because all conclusions about the observable world are in some measure, by comparison with mathematics, uncertain, therefore all are equally uncertain. We know what we mean by 'good evidence' when we are talking about murders, or the origin of an earthquake, or who won the Test Match. So let us concede with a good grace that Hume is not talking nonsense when he says that we have 'proof' that the sun will rise tomorrow, in at least one quite respectable sense of 'proof'. If a man were to come up to me this evening and seriously contend that there was a good chance that the sun wouldn't rise tomorrow, I would, unless he had information about an impending cataclysm, say a star passing over-close, be able to show him overwhelmingly good reasons why he was wrong.

2.17 But to admit this is not to admit that it is impossible that the sun should fail to come up tomorrow. Suppose we get up after the usual night's sleep and find no sun, and the world disordered and catastrophic about us – well, we have to face the fact, and we aren't involving ourselves in any self-contradiction.

2.18 So we have arrived at two conclusions. First, it is not impossible that something quite contrary to our previous experience should occur. Second, we have proof, in certain cases, that nothing contrary to our previous experience will occur. In short, we can have the best possible evidence there is that X will not occur; and yet X might conceivably after all occur.

2.19 And this shows that there is a paradox in what Hume says. For according to his argument he must fail to believe in a miracle, the violation of a law of nature; and yet on his general philosophical principles, experience being the sole guide, he cannot rule out the theoretical possibility that such an event should occur.

2.20 Imagine Hume being present at someone's rising from the dead. What does he say to himself? 'Impossible, gentlemen, impossible. This is contrary to all my previous experience of mortality, and to the testimony of countless human beings. It would be a lesser miracle that my eyes deceive me than that this resurrection should have occurred.' Well, perhaps of course his eyes do deceive him. Let him test them. Let him investigate minutely the resurrected body. Can he still doubt?

2.21 Nor does it help for someone to defend Hume as follows, by saying: 'There *may* be some perfectly natural explanation after all. Perhaps it's a kind of psychosomatic cure of death; you know how much the mind affects the body. Maybe one day we shall get round to understanding this sort of thing.' It is useless to say this, since, natural explanation or no, the event in question is quite contrary to previous experience. Nobody has seen this sort of thing happening, and lo! now it happens. On Hume's argument we have a proof that it cannot happen, and yet here it is happening. Better to disbelieve our eyes, however clear and eagle-like they may be.

2.22 Hume's general argument, then, fails. We cannot rule out *a priori*, i.e. without recourse to observing the way the world is, the possibility of miracles; and therefore we cannot frame a rule about believing in them which would rule out the legitimacy of believing what we see, if we were to see a miracle. But this by no means shows that we have solved all the problems about belief in miracles. For one thing, Hume's particular reasons for holding that we never have, as a matter of fact, clinching testimony of their occurrence (2.7) still remain. Again, there is a difficulty about saying that a miracle is a violation of a law of nature, as Hume's definition would have us describe it (2.5).

2.23 In regard to this latter problem, there is a preliminary paradox that assails us. As we have already seen, we conclude, on the basis that we always see that such-and-such happens, that such-and-such always happens (2.11). Formally, and crudely, we can express a law of nature as having the following shape: 'All A-events are followed by B-events' or more simply still as 'All As are Bs'. That the last is a simplified version of its predecessor can be seen by rewriting 'All A-events are followed by B-events' as 'All As have the property of being Bs' where to be a B is defined as 'being followed by a B-event'. Now the simplest variety of propositions of the form 'All As are Bs' are those like 'All tigers are quadrupeds' or 'All humans are rational animals' or 'All swans are white'. Now these have a simple logical feature, namely that they are contradicted by propositions of the form 'At least one A is not a B'—e.g. 'At least one tiger is not a quadruped', 'At least one human is not a rational animal' or 'At least one swan is not white'. Clearly, if these latter are true, the corresponding propositions of the form 'All As are Bs' are false; and conversely. It follows from this that in order to disprove a law of nature all you have to do is to produce an exception, a negative instance. Then the supposed law of nature turns out not to be a law of nature. How then can a miracle violate a law of nature? If it is an exception to it, then the law of nature is already (so to speak) destroyed. There seems then to be a paradox in the definition of miracle. The miracle seems for ever frustrated in its attempt to violate; for as soon as it imagines that it has succeeded, it finds that there was nothing there after all to violate! It is like someone trying to live in a state of conjugal bliss with a bachelor: for as soon as there is conjugality there is (by definition) no bachelor.

2.24 These remarks, incidentally, bring out two important points about laws of nature. First, the use of the word 'laws' when we talk of them is not a satisfactory analogy. For laws in the primary sense, when we speak about the laws enacted by Parliament or about moral laws, are such that, even if they are often broken, they do not thereby cease to be valid. But this is not, as we have seen, possible with a scientific law. Indeed, one might say that the whole point of legal and moral laws is that they get broken: were it not for the fact that many human beings are inclined to commit adultery there would be no point in having a commandment about it. We do not teach our children that it is morally wrong to strangle lions wantonly with their bare hands, for – so far as is known – no human being has the least inclination to do such a thing, wrong though it would be. That sin is attractive is thus, in a way, a necessary truth: for only the sweet fruits get forbidden. (Though we must remember, happily, that not *all* sweet fruits are forbidden.)

2.25 The second lesson we can learn from the foregoing (2.23) about scientific laws is that, formally at least, it seems easier to disprove them than prove them. We are not in a position to search out every tiger that has existed, now exists or will exist, to check on whether it is a quadruped. It is just that all the ones we have come across have this property. That all atoms have a certain constitution is something we could not possibly verify conclusively. The best we can do is to sample a small slice of the universe. Atoms and tigers are here 'open' rather than 'closed' classes. For 'All tigers are quadrupeds' has a logical difference from 'All my friends speak Chinese'. The latter statement might be true: George speaks Chinese, so does Henry, and Wong, and Abraham. . . . But I am not meaning to imply that anyone who joined my circle of friends would speak Chinese. I might get friendly with Giovanni, who speaks no Oriental tongue; and then it would no longer be true that all my friends speak Chinese. My friends are a 'closed' class, consisting of a finite and countable number of individuals. But when I say 'All tigers are quadrupeds' I am meaning to imply that tigers born tomorrow would be quadrupeds too. It means 'If anything is or were to be a tiger it would be a quadruped'. But 'All my friends are Chinese-speakers' does not entail 'If anyone were to be my friend, he would be a Chinese-speaker'. So then, in the case of scientific laws, which are about 'open' classes of events, we cannot be in a position to examine all the instances. We take a sample and go on that. So, then, a scientific law cannot be absolutely conclusively verified. But it can be conclusively falsified, if I find an exception, an indubitable exception, to it. For this reason, it has been argued by some philosophers of science (notably by Karl Popper) that a good scientific theory is not so much one which has been proved, as one which has survived disproof, and survived it not by cheating, by taking no risks of being falsified, but has survived it despite the fact that it has stuck its neck out.

2.26 To return, however, to our paradox (2.23). What are we to say? We could perhaps alter the definition of 'miracle' and allow that a miracle is not a violation of a law of nature. But this lands us in certain difficulties. We could, for example, treat a miracle simply as a sign – that is, as an event which shows something about God to men on a particular occasion, but which occurs in a natural sequence of events. But it could not be a sign unless it were something rather extraordinary. The fact that it rained at 2 o'clock this afternoon could scarcely function as a particular sign of God's dealings with men. Of course we may see in the rain something of the power of God, if we hold that he has created everything. But the whole point of saying that a miracle is a sign is that though God is associated with all things he is associated with some things more than others. And if an event, though bizarre, could be given a scientific or ordinary explanation, would it any longer retain its power of causing wonder in us? To the primitive mind a thunderstorm might seem to be caused by the direct action of a supernatural being. But now we know some meteorology we may admire the spectacle, but we do not see it as something to be especially moved and astonished by.

2.27 And to treat the miracle simply as a sign means that it has some special significance *for us*, though it is capable of being explained naturally. But this seems too 'subjective'. A miracle would depend on the way it strikes us. Unless the way it strikes us is controlled by something 'objective', miracles would cease to be *evidence* of anything. They would be illustrations of what we mean when we talk about God's activity; but there is a gap between meaning and truth. Would it really be God's activity we saw or just what we choose to call God's activity? It might be as if we were to say: 'All events involving blue things are special signs of God's activity.' Here we would certainly be given a *meaning* to the idea of God's activity; but so far nothing has been done to show that events involving blue things actually are the special effects of God's activity.

2.28 It might be more fruitful, if we can, to escape the paradox in another way. Could we somehow claim that a miracle has the peculiar property of violating but not destroying a law of nature, despite what we said about the deadly power of the negative instance? A digression upon the apparent villainy of the scientist might be useful here.

2.29 His apparent villainy arises out of his great reluctance to forfeit a law of nature, and this indeed is in line with Hume's advice about coming to a judgment about matters of fact (2.4). It is not to be thought that the scientist does an experiment, finds a result contrary to all his previous experience and then good-naturedly shrugs his shoulders, sighing 'And there goes another scientific law'. Rather he concludes that he must have made a mistake in his experiment. And anything bizarre tends to be treated in the same way. For instance, the usual reaction to the work of Professor Rhine on extra-sensory perception is 'There must be something wrong with his statistics': and perhaps indeed there is. Consequently, the serious-minded scientist, on finding his wretched and uncomfortable experimental result, not only treats his apparatus and methods with suspicion, but cogitates and repeats the experiment, checking up on it in new ways if he can. But if he and his colleagues keep on finding the same thing, then there is nothing for it but to reject the law. Or at least to tinker with it in some way so that it is made to correspond with the new finding. Thus the law is scrapped or, as we might say, changed; but it must be remembered that even if it is only changed, then strictly speaking it is, in its original form, scrapped. But only, as I say, with reluctance. The moral of this digression is that science is not just observational: it is experimental. Even astronomy, perhaps the least experimental of the major sciences, for you cannot put galaxies in laboratories, is considerably experimental – the physics of stars is investigated by reference to experimentally-checked laws found to obtain in our little corner of the cosmos, and moreover the subtlety and repeatability of many observations gives them an experimental character.

2.30 The fact that science is experimental is significant for our discussion. For experimentation involves controlled conditions and, thereby, repeatability. The great thing about an experiment is that it can be repeated. It is not, as we saw, the single experiment which produces the negative instance of deadly power. It is the repeated, the sifted, the scrutinized experiment which does this.

2.31 This implies that what we said about falsification (2.25) was greatly over-simplified. Or rather that our notion of a negative instance was over-simplified. We find now that the negative instance is not a single event but a repeatable event. In other words, it is a small-scale law of nature: it is described by something of the form 'Under these special conditions, that occurs'. The large-scale law of nature is supposed to apply to a number of particular *types* of situations: these are its instances, not single events. Suppose the law of gravitation (a large-scale law) implies that balls will roll down an inclined plane at a certain pace, given the mass of the earth, the angle of the plane, and so on. And suppose that the experiment always comes off as predicted: the small-scale law holds. And then suppose that one unfine day some new Galileo finds that we had not got the conditions as we thought we had, in their purity, and that some unseen factor always entered into our experiments. And suppose that we remove that factor and lo! the balls move at the wrong pace. Now we have a new small-scale law which is an exception, an anomaly. Now we have to scrap or modify, that is to scrap, the large-scale law.

2.32 The relevance of all this to miracles is readily apparent. Miracles are not experimental, repeatable. They are particular, peculiar events occurring in idiosyncratic human situations. They are not small-scale laws. Consequently they do not destroy large-scale laws. Formally, they may seem to destroy the 'Always' statements of the scientific laws; but they have not the genuine deadly power of the negative instance.

2.33 But we may well be unhappy at this solution to our paradox, and say: 'But in any given instance of a supposed miracle, the strange anomaly must be caused by some condition which we have overlooked. Still, granting that it isn't, but that inexplicably, contrary to all past and, no doubt, future experience, a man really rises from the dead, then this will be an uncaused event, a sudden bit of randomness in an otherwise orderly universe.' The trouble is that we seem to be in a cleft stick. Either all events are caused, in which case the violation of a law of nature seems to be ruled out; or we regard the miraculous as an uncaused – a random – event. But why should we attach any particular importance to random events?

2.34 But what is meant by saying that all events are caused? It is too general a statement to be refuted. For even if, in a given case, I cannot discover the cause of an event, it can always be said that one day, conceivably, somebody could discover some (unspecified) cause. How could one's claim that every event has a cause be ever brought to a clinching test? But the statement nevertheless does at least express our normal determination to seek for an explanation of anything puzzling which may turn up. Yet does someone who believes in miracles believe that there is no cause of such events? Does he really think of them as random occurrences? Of course not. For he holds that they have a supernatural cause. There is a great difference, in his eyes, between the merely random and the miraculous. It might be – given sufficient time – that the Thames might run uphill for an hour, just because by an extremely improbable chance all the molecules were pressing that way at the same time. But this event would have a very different flavour from the resurrection of Christ. The believer in miracles, then, does not deny that miracles are caused. But he says that they are the result of direct supernatural causation.

2.35 Yet this conception itself bristles with intellectual difficulties. First, when we explain an event, we normally refer to some law of nature. For instance, if the pond is frozen over, we explain that, not merely by reference to the prevailing conditions, but also by reference to the law that water freezes at 32° Fahrenheit. Can we refer to a like law in explaining an event as due to the direct action of God? Surely not, for there are no 'laws of supernature' open to our inspection.

2.36 Another difficulty, connected with this, is that when we speak of a cause and effect, ordinarily both are, in principle, observable. Suppose that I am walking down a hillside and see smoke rising near a railway track in the valley. Though I do not observe the train, I can infer its presence, as the cause of the smoke. But only because I have seen trains and smoke together in the past. And I can, moreover, check on my inference as I walk on, for when I come close I may be able to see the train itself. But God cannot be directly observed: so how do I know of any link between him and any observable event? To be sure of his being a cause, I would have to see him and the effect of his action together: only this, it seems, would establish the link.

2.37 Another difficulty is that scientific explanations have a predictive value. On the basis of them I can predict the future. Yet no predictions follow from my explanations in terms of God's direct action. From it follows no prediction, even a probable one, about similar action to follow in the future. Indeed it would seem impious to *expect* further miracles. (Though pilgrimages to Lourdes might be held to belie this judgment.)

2.38 The effect of the first difficulty (2.35) is much mitigated when we consider the case of the explanation of human actions. I explain why it is that George has suddenly sprung up from his chair by saying: 'He has just remembered that he is supposed to be at the station to meet his uncle Henry.' This has as its background the fact that he had promised to be there; and the underlying assumption of my explanation is that George normally keeps his promises. But it would be wrong to say that it is a law of nature that George keeps his promises. Sometimes, alas, he does not. Still, it has some analogy with a law: for we are referring to what normally happens. His promise-keeping is a facet of his character. His present action 'fits in' with much else in his behaviour. Could we say the same about a miracle? – that it 'fits in' with God's character? In a loose way I think we can, though there remains the difficulty, which we shall come to, of how we know anything about God's character. It seems possible to say, then, that a kind of explanation is being offered when we say that such-and-such an event is due to God's direct action. It links up the present event in an intimate way with the Creator, with religious experience elsewhere and outside this particular context, with much else that is, supposedly at least, known about God's actions in history. In short, the explanation attaches the event to a whole nexus of facts.

2.39 Yet the second difficulty (2.36) is more serious, for it raises the central question of all philosophy of religion – namely how we can have any knowledge of that which is transcendent, of that which is, in some sense, beyond space and time. But I shall not discuss this immediately; let us content ourselves with a few remarks on the notion of observation. For the objection turns on the belief that God, being transcendent, is unobservable. Now observation is where one perceives something through the senses, and it is in principle public – that is, more than one person can observe the same object at the same time. Thus a table can be observed, as can the contents of a Wilson cloud chamber. Of course, in its pregnant scientific sense the term 'observe' implies more. The astronomer observing Betelgeuse doesn't just pop out of bed in the middle of the night, have a look at it and go back to snugness again. He watches it with careful attention with a purpose in mind and instruments to hand. But at any rate, the objects of science are observable (by and large, though certain difficulties arise over entities like electrons, and in psychology): they are objects which can be publicly perceived. And where – as with electrons – there are difficulties, at least the relevant theory is tied to and checked by what can be observed. Hence there seems to be something 'unscientific' about a doctrine which appeals to that which cannot in principle be observed, namely to God.

2.40 But to this there are a number of replies. First, just as (2.14) there is a danger and absurdity in trying to fit all proofs into a mathematical straitjacket, so likewise it may be absurd to try to fit all knowledge into a physical-scientific straitjacket. It is by no means obvious in advance that all knowledge must be based upon public observation, still less that it could all be accommodated in a strictly scientific framework. It is true that we have a certain drive towards simplification and unification: so that there is an attraction about a philosophical theory which states that all knowledge must be of this one kind. But this drive of ours towards unification certainly constitutes no knock-down judgment and if experience is richer than theory permits, let theory suffer.

2.41 Second, we are aware of inner states (for instance that I am now imagining the Mediterranean) though these states are not publicly observable. For I am aware of what is in my mind's eye, though you can only have it described to you, or infer it. It would therefore be absurd to say that all states of reality are publicly observable.

2.42 Third, though 'observe' may be a word that does not fit the case, there may be a kind of *awareness* of God. Certainly religious people believe that this is possible and in particular that certain great figures in religious history – prophets and mystics, Jeremiah and Eckhart, St Paul and St John of the Cross – have had experience of God in a most powerful and intimate way. Now if such a claim is correct, there is something which can be called 'awareness of God', even if it is not like the usual public observations of trees, chairs and stars. But why should it be? Aristotle said that the mark of the educated man is that he expects that degree of precision which the subject-matter allows. We could extend his principle and say that the educated man expects the kind of evidence relevant to the subject-matter. We certainly do not expect that God should be observable, like a tree. Nor do we base this expectation on mere whim, or bring it forth to get out of a philosophical difficulty; but it derives from the testimony of great religious men, from the traditional and central concepts of religion, from the way in which revelation is supposed to come to us. It is no new doctrine. No man shall see (observe) God; but sometimes men may see (be aware of) God.

2.43 As to the third difficulty with which we were faced, in regard to the idea that God directly causes miracles (2.37), it is true indeed that a doctrine which explains miracles as due to God's action does not have any predictive value *in regard to further miracles*. Yet it might have predictive value in other contexts, regarding the course of history, for instance. By attaching a miracle to a whole network of doctrines, some of which concern the future (for instance, they concern what in human life conduces to salvation, to the vision of God, to grace and so forth), it implicates it in a 'theory' which does have predictive value – and to this extent there is an analogy with scientific explanation. We may conclude, then, that it is by no means absurd to speak of explanation when we claim that an event is due to God's direct action.

2.44 It is obvious from all this that the claim that an event is miraculous presupposes some kind of belief in God or the supernatural. As we have seen (2.34), the miraculous is more than the merely random, more than the merely (scientifically) inexplicable. But without the concept of God, and considered without relation to a miracle's religious context, it would seem to be merely a random or inexplicable event. There might then be two views of the same miraculous event, depending on the presuppositions and interests of the people investigating or contemplating it. From the strictly scientific point of view, the event would be merely inexplicable. From the religious standpoint it could be considered as directly caused by God.

2.45 We have been talking, though, as if it were a simple matter to say that an event was scientifically inexplicable. But how could we ever know that an event fell into this category? For we could never be absolutely sure that some new theory would not appear which would give us a means of explaining the event. All that we would be entitled to say, perhaps, would be 'Given the present state of knowledge, this event cannot be scientifically explained'. What once looked like miraculous healing might be accounted for by new advances in medicine (the phenomenon of psychosomatic disorders is much better appreciated nowadays). These remarks fit in with Hume's objection that miracles chiefly abound amid barbarous peoples (2.7): for clearly the more ignorant people are, the more events there will be which are inexplicable to them in terms of natural processes.

2.46 Nevertheless, it is not true that people are unacquainted with laws of nature. You don't need to have any scientific expertise to know that people do not rise from the dead, that water freezes when it gets very cold, that heavy objects tend to fall towards the earth, and so on. It is still possible to detect a 'violation' of the otherwise universal course of events, even if sometimes or often ignorant people may make mistakes. But the fact that a lot of reported miracles are spurious does not entail that all are. Supposing that miracles do occur, and given that they have a mysterious and inexplicable nature, it would be most likely that the genuine miracles would also become surrounded with a lot of spurious ones. All miracles are inexplicable to us, but not all events inexplicable to us are miracles.

2.47 But these points bring us back to Hume's original argument. Though its main point is not (as we have argued – 2.22) valid, it still has this force: that we should have very good evidence before accepting a report of a miracle. It might be useful to say something about the general nature of this evidence, not from the point of view of determining whether we actually have it, which would be an historical enquiry, but from the point of view of saying something about its general nature, about what kind of thing the historian would be looking for. First, miracles do not occur in the abstract, but in particular personal and historical situations (2.32). Perhaps a random event has just occurred at the top of Everest, a piece of snow rising inexplicably and hovering over the summit for ten minutes. But such an event has not the flavour of the genuine miracle. This is because, in Western religious thought at least, the miracle has the characteristic of conveying to us something about God: it is a form of his self-disclosure. Thus it occurs in the context of a personal situation, and one which has a special religious significance. Thus one has to understand the religious context of the event, as well as having to presuppose the existence of a supernatural Being capable of causing the miraculous (2.44). It is the conjunction of the random and inexplicable event (looking at it merely from the scientific standpoint) with the religious context that constitutes the greatest wonder of all. If we really do find that a holy Teacher performs the inexplicable, it is a tremendous coincidence. Yet it is the fact that people are, in such contexts, more inclined to expect miracles than elsewhere that may make us suspicious of the empirical evidence. Consequently, the historian who investigates the New Testament may well feel that such plausibility as attaches to the accounts of the resurrection arises from the other events of Christ's life and of the lives of the Apostles, rather than that the authenticity of Christ's claims and of those of his followers is seen from this miracle.

2.48 Yet this itself seems to raise a vital problem about history. If the Christian claims that his faith is historical, he may mean one of two things. He may mean that it centres upon events which he believes occurred at a certain point in history; or he may mean that his faith can be validated by historical enquiry. For there are two senses of 'history': first, the sequence of human events; second, the enquiry bearing upon them known in schools and universities as 'history'. In the first sense, you can record history; in the second sense you can *do* it. It may be useful to introduce some terminology to make this distinction clear. When we say that an event belongs to the sequence of events, we shall call it 'historical'. And let us use 'metahistorical' to refer to the type of enquiry pursued by the historian, when he tries to find out what the sequence of events was. Now in the first sense Christianity is historical, or claims to be, for Christ's life belonged to the sequence of human events; but what of the second sense? Would the objective and 'scientific' historian, in reading the New Testament, be willing to concede that the miraculous might have occurred, that, metahistorically, it could be proved? It is one thing to agree, as the result of the kind of philosophical argument which we have been pursuing, that in *theory* a resurrection from the dead is possible. It is quite another thing to take this merely theoretical possibility into one's reckoning. In theory, it is conceivable that the Celtic saint who is recorded as having walked across the water from Ireland to Wales did in fact do so. Miracles can happen. But we would be rightly suspicious of a modern historian who set this event down as a fact.

2.49 Furthermore, it so happens that, as a result of researches over the last hundred years, Biblical scholars have opened up a large number of critical questions as to how much of the record of Jesus' life contained in the Gospels represents fact. Thus questions arise far beyond the sphere of the recorded miracles. Moreover, it is also clear that some of the concepts used by the Biblical writers are out-

moded in the light of modern knowledge: thus the assumption that
the universe is 'three-decker' (so that going to heaven means literally
ascending upwards) must be scrapped. This in turn throws doubt
upon certain narratives; consider, for instance, Christ's ascension
into heaven. Why did he go *upwards*? For such reasons, Biblical
scholars may be inclined to despair of being sure that they can paint
an accurate picture of the historical Jesus. Such a despair has had
a philosophical effect, in tempting the theologian to concentrate
upon the contemporary significance of Christ rather than on his
actual historical life – so that the historical Jesus tends to be
replaced by the Christ met with in 'existential' encounter, the Christ
who is experienced by the faithful. A notable representative of this
trend is Rudolf Bultmann. But it is liable to destroy essential
Christianity. For the Christian has always had to hold two things
together: belief in the work of the historical Jesus; and belief in
the continuing possibility of communion and encounter with Christ.
The historical and the experiential must be seen together as com-
plementary parts of his faith. For if the historical does not matter,
then the Gospel narratives become mere myths, and the Incarnation
is meaningless.

2.50 Now there is no doubt that it is hard for the Christian to
claim that the central facts of the Christ's career can be metahistorically validated. As we have seen, the objective historian may
be unwilling to allow the real possibility of the miraculous, only
conceding a theoretical possibility. Further, the work of Christ, his
atoning sacrifice, has a cosmic significance which goes well beyond
the historical event of a man's dying on the cross in such-and-such
circumstances. More generally, Christ's divinity, though it requires
metahistorical backing, cannot be established simply on the basis
of metahistorical enquiry. For example, his being in some sense one
with the Father presupposes belief in the Father, and this is not
just a belief about history: God the Father may intervene in history,
but he is not an historical figure. For these reasons, one cannot have
metahistorical proof of the truth of Christianity.

2.51 But this does not at all entail that we can reformulate Christianity in such a way that the historical events can be left out. It may

be hard to show convincingly in an 'objective' manner that Christ
rose from the dead, but *our* difficulties do not prevent him from
having done so. Nor does the fact that we cannot gain such a
metahistorical proof of, say, the resurrection imply that the Christian
historian, more willing than his agnostic brother to entertain the real
possibility of the miraculous, is thereby metahistorically disreputable.
If there are grounds for thinking Jesus divine despite the inadequacy
of our records, it would be foolish to rule out in advance the possibility that he rose from the dead. The Christian historian may be
taking a gamble on the facts: but he may after all turn out to be
right.

2.52 So far we have been considering the difficulties that the
historian and the scientist might feel. But there is a difficulty about
miracles from the side of theology. It is this. If God is creator of
the cosmos and it is good, what need is there for him to interfere
with its processes? And for that matter, if somehow the creation has
gone bad, why does he not interfere more often? Feeding the five
thousand was good, but there are five hundred million or more who
are hungry today.

2.53 We must recall that the primary context of a miracle is supposed to be God's self-disclosure. Now on the theistic view, and in
particular on the Christian view, the essential goodness of the cosmos is reflected in its independence, and the goodness of men, not
their moral goodness so much as their value as separate entities
and as particular individual beings, is reflected in their freedom and
autonomy. Neither the cosmos nor humans are pieces of puppetry
or thin illusions. Indeed the distinction which we draw between
natural processes and the miraculous where God intervenes directly
implies that natural causes have their own efficacy. Now if the
cosmos is independent in this way, it is distinct from God. And if it
is distinct from God it does not directly show God: indeed it mostly
hides God. But yet if God is to show himself, he must sometimes
remove the veil that the cosmos constitutes, and break through the
natural processes. But to break through all the time would be to
destroy them and to mislead men, for the strangeness of the miraculous and its rarity reflect the otherness and transcendence of God.

To be always breaking through would constitute a cheapening of the vision of God that the miracle provides. This (crudely) is the answer to the first question.

2.54 But some may cavil at the assertion that the cosmos is independent and autonomous. For does not the doctrine of creation, properly understood, imply that the universe is dependent on God? Would it not vanish in the twinkling of an eye if he were to withdraw his support? It is clear that some distinction must be made, and as follows.

2.55 Though God is undoubtedly (according to Christian doctrine) that upon which the cosmos is totally dependent, nevertheless the cosmos has its own separate characteristics and patterns of activity. Suppose I build a machine: now though I have created it and though I can stop it working any time I wish, say by smashing it up with a hammer, the machine has a certain independence just because of its regular manner of functioning, its regular pattern of characteristics. Suppose I interfere continually, making this cog move that cog now and another cog in a second's time, I would end with, not a machine, but a chaos of parts. Supposing further that through some wizardry I can keep altering the properties of the various parts, making this cog soft and yellow now, hard and purple in a second's time, and so on. I would no longer have a determinate thing; but just a certain area of chaos. There would be nothing left which was a separate object which I had created: or at most the most evanescent doodle, a kind of flickering extension of my fingers. Thus to speak of a separate and independent thing (in this sense) is to speak of something which has its own pattern of characteristics and activities. But if there is a pattern, we can trace out its connexions: this occurs, then that. This event is the immediate cause of that, even if the machine is totally created by me. Thus the notion of the independence of the cosmos is closely allied to the regularities exhibited by it. And this notion of independence is not inconsistent with the idea that the cosmos is ultimately dependent for its existence and continued functioning upon God's will.

2.56 As to the subsidiary question about the feeding of the millions (2.52), this belongs to a discussion of the problem of evil (6.1ff.), and with this we are not directly concerned at the moment (not all problems can be tackled at once).

2.57 Finally, let us look at the solution to the problem of miracles which has been proposed here, and consider what it implies about scientific laws and about causation. For a view about the nature of causes is rather central to any general philosophical theory, and indeed it was Hume's treatment of it that led to Kant's attempt to frame an alternative picture. Our solution, then, briefly is this. There is no reason in the nature of things why occasional random and inexplicable events should not occur. There is, and here we agree with Hume, no absolute necessity why things should always continue to operate in the way in which they have in the past. Thus we cannot rule out in advance the possibility that the miraculous, which is meant to be scientifically inexplicable, may occur. But supposing such an event does happen, it is not sufficient reason to abandon the natural law that the miracle has 'violated'. For what we mean by a genuine negative instance (the one which has the deadly power of destroying the law) is an experimentally repeatable exception. But the miracle does not fall into this category – otherwise it would itself be a new small-scale law, not a 'violation' of regularity. But the miracle differs from the merely random in having a supposed unobservable cause (namely God) though from the purely scientific point of view it would look random. Of course, one would have to have good reason for rejecting the hypothesis that after all the event may have an explanation (for does not science progress?); but in certain cases one might have practical assurance that it was inexplicable; e.g. if a person after the onset of physical decay genuinely rose to bodily life again. Such then is the general view that has been presented here. But it implies that we would not have to take scientific laws strictly as asserting 'Whenever A then B', but rather as saying that 'There is an overwhelming tendency for an A to be followed by a B'. In other words 'Every event must have a cause' (a principle which intuitively we feel must hold, as a presupposition of scientific enquiry) is suspect. If it means 'Every event must of necessity fit into a pattern of regularities' it is false, even if we may use it in practice as a principle to guide our investigations.

That we can so use it follows from the way in which we have interpreted the negative instance: for the random variety has no implications for the future, while the deadly exception (being a small-scale law) does. Thus all events which can be checked upon in a scientific manner can be found to fit into patterns of regularities. The merely random, because it does not repeat itself, can safely be neglected.

2.58 Further, though the miraculous does not fit into a pattern of observable regularities, it is believed to have a supernatural cause. So that from the religious point of view it is not a causeless event. But one could only appeal to this idea of a supernatural cause if it is legitimate to believe in such a transcendent Being. We shall have to come later to this all-important question. But we can in the meantime note that it follows, from the view about miracles which has here been expressed, that miracles by themselves could not serve as conclusive evidence of a divine revelation. For, as we saw (2.44), one needs a prior acceptance and understanding of the idea of God, and not just an abstract belief in him, but a knowledge in some degree of his character (2.38). A miracle, then, is not an external guarantee of the truth of revelation, but belongs with a pattern of revelation – a pattern of divine self-disclosure.

2.59 Our discussion of miracles has taken us into the heart of the philosophical problem of causation. But it is not just in regard to miracles that there is an apparent conflict between science and other beliefs: for also the notion that events are determined by laws has often been taken to suggest that there is no place for human freedom. This, as we shall see, was one of the main problems which Kant attempted to solve.

3

Kant and Human Freedom

3.1 IT would of course be absurd to try to give in a brief space an adequate account of Immanuel Kant's difficult and complex philosophical thinking. But there are certain strands of his thought which are of profound interest to the philosopher of religion, and indeed the idea of causation (2.9), which has figured prominently in our discussion of miracles, is closely involved in the three main aims of Kant's philosophy.

3.2 First, Kant wanted to see how natural science is possible, given Hume's embarrassing arguments and the problem of induction (2.10, 2.11). The rise of Newtonian physics, a splendid and powerful achievement, seemed to imply two things. First, being based upon observation and experiment, it suggested that knowledge must be based upon perception. Second, in its fruitful ordering of reality and in its capacity to see mathematical relations between events, it suggested that reality is naturally intelligible and orderly, and that the relation between cause and effect must have a kind of inner necessity. Hume stressed the former suggestion, and in so doing produced a radically empiricist account of the world – all knowledge being derived ultimately from sense-impressions. But in so doing he destroyed the notion of inner necessity and orderliness in reality. 'Upon the whole,' he wrote, 'there appears not, throughout all nature, any one connexion which is conceivable by us. All events seem entirely loose and separate. One event follows another; but we never can observe any tie between them.' It seemed as if the empirical element in science swallowed up and destroyed the rational element. Kant wanted to prevent this, and to solve the problem posed by Hume. How indeed is natural science possible?

3.3 The second main aim of Kant was to put metaphysics on a proper footing. Hitherto, philosophers had tended to produce arguments about ultimate reality, the existence of God, and so on, without being *critical*. That is to say, they had not first of all scrutinized in a critical manner the nature and limitations of human reason. The result was, according to Kant, that metaphysics went on being landed in contradictions. Two of these contradictions – or *antinomies*, as Kant called them – are of special significance to us here, and both involve the notion of causes. First, philosophers (so Kant thought) can prove that everything in the world takes place solely in accord with natural laws: but also that there are some uncaused causes, since there is free will. Second, they can prove that the world must depend upon a self-existent Being (a Being that depends upon nothing else for its existence), and also that no such Being can exist. When we meet such mutually contradictory proofs, Kant argues, we can conclude that philosophers, at least part of the time, are arguing illegitimately, and not so much because the 'proofs' are technically invalid, as that they are somewhere or other using reason beyond its proper scope. It is like the case of the soccer enthusiast watching rugby for the first time. He sees a player lift the ball with his hands, and concludes that he has committed a foul; and yet he notices that the referee has not blown his whistle, and so concludes that the player has *not* committed a foul. He runs into this contradiction because he has been using the concepts of association football uncritically. He has not asked whether he is using these concepts beyond their proper sphere. Kant, then, wishes to examine the nature and limitations of reason as employed in metaphysics.

3.4 The first of the two antinomies mentioned above throws light on the third main aim of Kant's philosophy, namely the proper description of the nature of moral action and of its relation to other spheres of experience. How could morality (with its central presupposition that there is free will) be reconciled with science (with its central presupposition that every event must have a cause)?

3.5   The discussion of these points can conveniently be divided into two parts. First, we can see how problems about causation bear upon human freedom. And second, we can consider how Kant's critical examination of reason led to his rejection of the classical arguments for the existence of God, a rejection which has been profoundly influential.

3.6   Whereas Hume started, in a radically empiricist manner, from sense-impressions, and attempted to confine our knowledge of the world to what could be derived from them, Kant was too keenly aware of the apparently disastrous consequences to science of taking up such a position. For him, sense-impressions are not enough. To have objective knowledge – knowledge which goes beyond a flux of sensations – certain concepts or categories, for instance the category of causality, must be applied to the sense-impressions. These categories are not derived from sense-experience, and they apply indifferently to all kinds of sense-impressions; and so they can be termed *a priori*, i.e. they are 'prior' to any particular experience of the world. They are concepts which the understanding brings to bear in trying to disentangle and make orderly the sense-impressions with which the world confronts us. Indeed, properly speaking, we could not have any perceptions at all without such concepts. For when I say that I see something, and am not just having certain subjective experiences, I am claiming something objective above reality. I am already in some degree understanding that reality. Without the use of the category of substances or *things*, we could only speak of a chaos of sense-impressions; without the idea of causality we could have no understanding of the way the world works. The world throws up, as it were, a kaleidoscope of impressions: the mind, so to say, gives them order. The two ingredients are necessary for knowledge.

3.7   The trouble with some philosophers, Kant holds, is that they attempt to use these categories or concepts beyond the limits of experience. Thus tracing out causes indefinitely leads to the idea that behind them all lies a First Cause (i.e. God). But if this Cause be the cause of the whole world then it is by definition cause of everything that is or could be given in experience. But then the First Cause must lie *outside* all possible experience. But then we are illegitimately using the notion of cause beyond its proper sphere, and one of the necessary ingredients of knowledge is absent. No wonder contradictions and antinomies arise! But of this we shall speak later, in discussing Kant's criticisms of the arguments for the existence of God.

3.8 It is implicit in the use of the categories, according to Kant, that we make certain general judgments about the world. Thus it is implied in the use of the concept *cause* that every event must have a cause: and it is this which generates the difficulty about moral freedom. Now, as we have argued earlier (2.10), Hume seems right in holding that it is always in principle possible that any given causal law may cease to hold tomorrow, that the random is always in principle possible. Nevertheless, Kant is still correct to see that there is some kind of conflict between science and morality. For, first, though we may agree that random events are always *theoretically* possible, this is not to say that they actually occur in any given context. There is nothing in Hume's point to show that any actual beings, such as humans, are exempt from causal regularities. Indeed, modern advances in cybernetics and brain-physiology must be thought to suggest that mankind is on the threshold of elaborating such a science of human behaviour.

3.9 It might be replied to this that modern physics already indicates a vast area where strict causation does not occur: where indeed there is a strong element of randomness. This area is that covered by sub-atomic physics. But it is only microscopic events, events which occur on a very tiny scale, where the element of randomness enters in. For large-scale events, the situation is different, and classical determinism seems still to hold good. Now we have no special reason to hold that microscopic indeterminacy plays any important role in human behaviour. Men are big entities, and from the point of view of physics, so are brain-cells.

3.10 But even supposing there were random elements which entered into the causes of human action, this would scarcely help us in the problem of free will. Suppose I decide to go and watch cricket: and suppose that my decision depends upon some random prior event, for instance an unpredictable movement of an electron deep in my brain: can I call my decision a free one? Randomness is the way the cat jumps, not genuine choice. Hence, whether human actions are determined by prior causes according to natural laws, or whether they are merely random events, free will in any genuine sense seems impossible.

3.11 We may then be tempted to ask whether belief in free will is really necessary. Yet, as Kant affirmed, 'ought' implies 'can'. That is to say, if I cannot do X, it cannot be true that I ought to do X. It could not possibly be my duty to fly to Alpha Centauri tomorrow, since no space craft has been built which is capable of this feat – and anyway I wouldn't possess one myself. If someone tells me, 'You ought to have gone to see your Aunt Ethel off at the station', it is a reasonable reply, which rebuts the 'ought', to say 'I was held up in the traffic and couldn't get there in time'. Only if I *can* do X is it in order to say that I *ought* to do X. It is a necessary condition of my having a duty or obligation that I am in a position to fulfil it. I can be blamed for failing to do what I could have done and ought to have done. Likewise I can be praised for doing a duty which I might not have done. But I would not be due any praise if I had no choice but to do it, if I could *not* do it. So just before a praiseworthy or blameworthy action, two propositions would be true: 'I can do it' and 'I can fail to do it'. Thus moral action implies that one has a choice.

3.12 But (it is often argued) if all my actions are the result of prior causes, then a particular action is such that no other result could have occurred. If I was caused to go and watch cricket today, then there was no other (real) choice open to me. It seems then that morality, which presupposes that my actions are free, and causal determinism are incompatible.

3.13 However, it has recently been argued by some philosophers that the appearance of incompatibility is misleading. The argument is, briefly, as follows.

3.14 (1) What we ordinarily mean by 'free' is 'not subject to external or internal constraint'. For instance, I am not free on a particular occasion if someone is holding a gun at me and telling me what to do. This is an instance of external constraint. Nor am I free if, because of being a kleptomaniac, I steal something from a shop. I am partially insane, and so suffering from internal constraint. This definition of freedom corresponds very roughly with the legal definition of responsible behaviour. Let us therefore call this notion of freedom 'juridical freedom'. It certainly seems to cover a lot of our every-day uses of the term 'free'. (2) Juridical freedom does not so far imply that my free actions are uncaused, but only that they are not the result of certain kinds of causes. (3) Further, to say an action is caused is merely to bring it into a pattern of regularities: it is to say that given all the facts it could have been predicted. As a matter of fact we are very ignorant of the causal laws affecting human beings, so that it is most often hazardous to attempt predictions. But in *principle* they could be predicted (says this kind of determinist). Thus 'All human actions are the result of prior causes' means 'All human actions are predictable in principle'. (4) But to say that an action could be predicted is compatible with saying that it is not subject to internal or external constraint, that is, with saying that it is free (in the juridical sense). For instance, a friend of mine is faced with either steak or tunny-fish. Knowing his dislike of the latter I accurately predict that he will choose the steak. Does this make him unfree? Was I forcing him to choose it? Was his choice the consequence of guns or lunacy? Clearly not. Ergo, freedom and determinism are compatible.

3.15 This doctrine would affect our views about morality for the following reason. The whole point of the juridical distinction between free and unfree arises because unfree actions are those which could not have been changed by punishment, reward, praise or blame. I do not blame the kleptomaniac because it will do no good, whereas the ordinary thief can be shamed into virtue, perhaps. Thus praise and blame, and so forth, have simply a utilitarian or engineering function; they are to be used for engineering good behaviour. We smack the child to make him good: we blame adult actions to improve the moral tone. Thus moral judgments are not important *in themselves* (as people often think) but only for the results that they may have. Clearly, on such a view it will be impossible to think of punishment as simply being retributive, as giving the bad man his due. This taken by itself does no good, and only increases the amount of avoidable suffering in the world. The point of punishment must be to deter or to reform. Similar remarks should apply to rewards: and all this may affect our view of heaven and hell. For what point, unless we believe in retribution, does eternal punishment have? (6.47).

3.16   But this doctrine of the compatibility of free will and determinism, an earlier version of which was dismissed rather contemptuously by Kant, has its difficulties. For suppose that a person is choosing between a wrong and a right action, say A and B. Let us imagine that he chooses A. While he is deliberating, before actually choosing A, he is (juridically) free to do both A and B, inasmuch as 'He does A' and 'He does B' are both compatible with physical laws of nature together with facts about his body and environment, and both are compatible with general facts about his psychology (he has no 'block' against doing either). Nevertheless, according to the compatibility theory, the outcome of his deliberation is predictable. There is, therefore, a further sense of 'psychologically impossible' in which it is psychologically impossible for him to choose B. Just as it is physically impossible, given the laws of nature and present conditions, for the moon to fly away into orbit round Mars, so it is somewhat similarly impossible for him to choose B.

3.17   It seems then unjust to blame him for choosing A. It would be irrational at least for him to feel guilt about doing A: the only relevant attitude would be a determination not to do things like A in future. Yet either he forms such a determination or he does not; and if he does not, how can he be blamed for *that*? We appear to be left in a situation where statements of the form 'You ought to do X' and 'It would be wrong not to do X' do not strictly apply to particular situations. Given their 'engineering' function, they are tools for improving men; but they do not state truths. Then how can I take them seriously? For only if I believe that it is true that I have an obligation, here and now, to do B can I allow this thought to enter into my deliberations. Only if it is true can the statement have its engineering function.

3.18 This seems to imply that the language of morals would have to be more radically refashioned than we thought, given the compatibility theory. It would no longer be correct to talk about particular obligations, but only about desirable states of affairs. That X is a desirable state of affairs is something, perhaps, which may enter into my deliberations when I am choosing a course of action; e.g. I might recognize that others' happiness would be promoted if I were to do B rather than A. And yet how can such a thought have weight with me unless I recognize an obligation to promote the happiness of others? And not just an obligation in the sense that it would be desirable if people were to obey it, but more intimately an obligation to promote happiness which is laid upon me in particular. I must feel 'That is what I ought to aim for'. It seems necessary that the individual must have a sense of obligation. Yet how is this compatible with recognizing that, if after all I fail to carry out the obligation, I was not to blame?

3.19 But it may be replied that I am here confusing determinism with fatalism. Determinism merely states that my actions are in principle predictable: fatalism says more – that, whatever I do, what will be will be. But the latter is patently false, for what will be is partly determined by what I do.

3.20 Yet there is probably a reason (other than mere confusion) why determinism gets interpreted in a somewhat fatalistic way. And the reason no doubt is this: that the recognition of truth plays an important part in the causation of human actions; and the compatibility theory, by taking the sting out of the notion of obligation, would, if thought to be true, affect the way in which we act. Thus though it ought not to make strict fatalists of us, it would tend to dry up the springs of moral action.

3.21 The fact that awareness of the truth is an element in the causes of human action sets men apart from the physical world. For the moon does not know what the sun is doing while she pursues her round, and the clock ticks blindly, unaware of time. To describe the causes of human action one has to bring in consciousness and awareness, for without these, how can there be purposes, intentions and the like? In fact, there is a double distinction here between men and the moon. For, first, men have conscious experiences, while the moon does not. This indeed is one of the facts which creates a great puzzle about men, and for that matter (no doubt) about some animals. For experiences appear to be of a different order from physical events; and yet obviously the two are closely interwoven – the pin stuck into my arm (a physical event) causes me pain (a psychological event). But where are my feelings, or the images which flit through my mind? We talk as though they perhaps occur in the head: and yet what sense does it make to say that my mental picture of the Battle of Waterloo is two inches from my right ear? And again, when a surgeon cuts my brain open, he sees grey cells but not my experience of seeing the operating theatre. In any ordinary sense, my experiences do not seem to be in space and time, though they may be of what is in space and time. This, then, is perplexing: for how do we account for the interactions between experiences and physical events?

3.22 But further, not only do we have experiences, while the moon does not, but we are aware of ourselves, aware, often enough, of what we are doing, and so forth. Perhaps this differentiates men even from the conscious animals. This ability to 'stand back' (as it were) and view ourselves and the world about us enables us to solve problems, whether of conduct or of an intellectual or artistic nature – to deliberate, calculate, cogitate. Any account, then, of human behaviour must take account of these facts of consciousness and of awareness.

3.23 But conscious, rational deliberation, and indeed thinking in general, does not follow a simple sequence, as though when I think of A and then B and then C, A is the cause of B and B of C. For A, B and C can have a kind of logical connexion, an internal link. As when a bowler bowls first the first ball of the over, then the next, and so on till the sixth, the first is not strictly the cause of the second and so on, likewise rational processes are brought together in coherent wholes, and the rational person can be aware of the pattern of his activity. This is one reason why, if we model the idea of 'cause' on what happens in physical nature, it can be very misleading to suggest that human actions are the results of prior causes. For at once we seem landed with a kind of physiological determinism, as though all my thoughts and deeds are the consequences of bodily (and, in particular, brain) states.

3.24 Nevertheless, modern advances in medicine, in brain physiology, in the theory and practice of computing machines – all these tend to make us think about the mind in physiological terms. Yet there is a paradox about it. For we distinguish between experiences and physical states; and then the thesis of physiological determinism turns out to involve the following: that all conscious states are caused by physiological states, even though the former can be distinguished from the latter. On a simplified model, what would happen is this: brain-state 1 (B1, we'll call it) causes state 1 (C1, we'll call it); and B2 causes C2; and so on. But what is the cause of B2? If we say that C1 is, then physiological determinism would amount just as much to the theory that bodily states are dependent upon conscious states as to the converse. It would no longer be physiological determinism in the proper sense. Hence B2 must be caused by B1. Thus we get a series B1, B2, B3 . . . Bn, which constitutes the genuine causal series. Thrown off by this causal sequence would be a lot of impotent side-effects, namely C1, C2, C3 . . . Cn. Consciousness would be a pointless by-product. But this is paradoxical, for (1) we account for actions partly by reference to conscious events and states and (2) how is it that evolution has produced this peculiarly trivial by-product (yet one by which men distinguish themselves from most other beings)?

3.25 The only way out of this paradox for physiological determinism is for it to deny the distinction between conscious and physiological states, to assert that *conscious states just are brain-states*. (This doctrine we can call 'physiological materialism'.) Then the sequences would be of the form B/C1, B/C2 . . . B/Cn. Conscious states would still be part causes of actions and evolution would have produced no trivial by-product, but the brain itself. This would appear to be the only plausible kind of materialism. But then how is it that we distinguish between conscious and bodily states? How is it that it is so natural to make this distinction? How are there two languages . . . the language about consciousness and the language about grey cells?

3.26 The physiological materialist would have to say something like this – that there can well be two systems of concepts (two kinds of language) both referring to the same thing. When a football goes into a net, this event can be described in purely physical terms (about the path of a body of such-and-such a size, of spherical shape, made of leather, etc.). But it can also be described by using the concepts of football: a goal has been scored. Do we really want to say that because there are two languages, there are two distinct events? Likewise, perhaps, the language of conscious experiences and the language of brain-cells are alternative ways of talking about the same events.

3.27 But why is it possible to speak in this double way about the football? What makes it appropriate to describe it in terms of the game is that the surrounding circumstances are right – twenty-two players on the field, a referee, the rules operative, no off-side infringement. A chunk of leather can be propelled into a net without there being a game of football, still less a goal scored. But still, the circumstances themselves have a peculiar character: they do not consist simply of twenty-three pieces of organized flesh on a stretch of grass. Because consciously a game of football is being played, according to certain conventions, and invested with significance by human beings, because of all this one can speak of a goal scored. But this in turn means that the distinction between the goal scored and the chunks of leather in the net, which we were using to illustrate the two forms of language about experiences and brain-cells, itself *depends on this very distinction* between the conscious and the physical. The same goes for other examples we might use, saying that a lightning flash is at once a white streak of light and an electricity discharge; or that a signal can be described in human or in purely physical terms.

3.28 Perhaps the physiological materialist would do better to say that somehow experiences and brain-states are two *aspects* of the same thing: the same event looks different when approached through different avenues of knowledge. But how can it look different unless it has characteristics which can be distinguished? But if it has, then we are back with saying that conscious states differ from physical ones. If a mountain looks blue from one angle and green from another and not because of my bad eyes, then there must be some objective difference between the two aspects of the mountain.

3.29 Nevertheless, the physiological materialist can reply that, for all our philosophical difficulties, brain physiology is progressing. Consider physics: whereas the ordinary man describes tables as solid and brown, the physicist has a whole new and illuminating language about atoms and the like. Similarly, there is the common-sense language which we ordinarily use about persons: but there is (or will be) also the refined scientific language of lobes and rhythms and cells.

3.30 It is instructive to pursue the parallel with physics, for it illustrates a difficulty in physiological materialism. Physics replaces the common-sense language of physical objects like tables with a language making much use of such theoretical concepts as *atom*, *electron* and so on. But these theoretical concepts have to be related to reports of observations; but the language of observation itself involves the use of expressions standing for experiences. Thus physics, though for particular purposes it may replace common-sense language with a refined scientific language, cannot dispense with the former. Likewise, physiological materialism could not dispense with the language of experiences. How then can it interpret the latter in its refined language about lobes and rhythms? In brief, to be a scientific theory it requires to use language about experiences; but the contents of the theory entail that the latter language can be replaced.

3.31 A further difficulty arises from the notion of 'two avenues of knowledge'. For the direct avenue (whereby we are aware of experiences) leads, on the theory, to the same place that the indirect brain physiological avenue leads. This implies that what I am aware of is a state of my brain. And yet this is peculiar, for I am not aware that it's my brain I'm aware of. But how can I be said to be aware of something which I am not aware of? The difficulty can be removed by saying that it's quite possible to be aware of something and yet not know what it really is. It is said that the inhabitants of Tierra del Fuego, on first seeing a European sailing ship, replete with masts and spars and rigging and what-not, couldn't make head or tail of it. It was a sort of incomprehensible mess to them. Yet they were looking at it. They were aware of something while not knowing what it really was. Likewise I could be aware of a patch of blue (say) without realizing that the sense-impression was really a state of my brain.

3.32 But this introduces a further difficulty. For do we not think of the blueness as belonging in some way to the object out there, which we are perceiving? How can the object of my awareness be both the state of my brain and the bit of sea I can glimpse two miles away from me and my brain? We might get over this difficulty by saying: 'But the sense-impression is the brain-state, though what I perceive is the sea'. It would then be on the basis of sense-impressions that I make objective judgments of perception, objective judgments about the external world. But this would seem to imply that all I am directly aware of is sense-impressions, or brain-states. I am never aware of the external world as such. The 'real' world out there is something which I never have experience of. How, then, can I know that my sense impressions (or brain-states) correspond to it? This is like the difficulty we ran into about God as the unobservable cause of miracles (2.36).

3.33 These are some of the difficulties, then, which physiological materialism runs into. These objections, however, are not absolutely 'knock-down' ones, and they are partly based on intuitive ideas which we have at present, which themselves might have to be revised if physiological materialism were true. Further, the theory is in part a prediction about the way that science will go, and it is not for the philosopher to be over-confident about prophesying the future of science. Nevertheless I shall assume that the theory is false, and that we have to make some kind of genuine distinction between mental and bodily states. It was well that we went into the matter in some detail, though; for the truth of religion depends on the assumption that one can have experience of the transcendent (whether it be nirvana or God). And it would seem to make little sense to suppose that this would be possible, except in a miraculous fashion, if physiological materialism were true. For if the theory were true, it would be tempting to conclude that since our experiences are caused by things in time and space, they cannot have as their object some state or Being which is *outside* space and time.

3.34 Nevertheless, even if we make the kind of distinction suggested, determinism, but not of a physiological sort, might still be true. For human actions might still be the results of prior causes, even if those causes include psychological ones. Thus Kant's problem may still be with us. Certainly he, though distinguishing psychology as a science from the physical sciences, thought that it was. What kind of a solution, then, did he attempt to give?

3.35 Since, according to Kant, all phenomena come under the principle that every event must have a cause (3.8), free will cannot be a phenomenon: it cannot be given in experience. It is nevertheless a presupposition of the moral law, which we apprehend. Thus it must exist, and yet it cannot be experienced. Man is not free, considered as a phenomenon: so he must be free considered in some other way. What other way, though, is there? Kant had already argued in the *Critique of Pure Reason* that the understanding of phenomena implied that these appearances in some sense derived from underlying entities. The latter Kant dubbed things-in-themselves. That such things-in-themselves exist is evident, for I could have no idea of myself, no consciousness of my own existence, without being aware that there are things outside me; there would otherwise be nothing with which I could contrast myself. But though things-in-themselves give rise to appearances, they cannot be themselves apprehended. We could have no empirical knowledge of them, for by definition they underlie appearances or phenomena, and only the latter can enter into a system of scientific knowledge. Thus things-in-themselves are unknowable, though their existence is assumed. Such entities Kant called *noumena* or intelligible entities, objects of the understanding, by contrast with phenomena. He thought that it was legitimate to speak of them, since the concept of a *noumenon* is free from self-contradiction. (And yet his use of the concept in the *Critique of Pure Reason* does seem to involve a contradiction, for he speaks of noumena as *giving rise* to phenomena. But this implies that we can apply the category of causality to something lying beyond appearances, beyond phenomena (3.7).)

3.36   Kant uses the notion of the noumenon to solve the free-will problem. Man as phenomenon is caused; but as noumenon (as an intelligible entity) he is free. As he says: 'The whole chain of appearances with respect to anything which concerns the moral law depends on the spontaneity of the subject as a thing-in-itself. Of the nature of this spontaneity, however, a physical explanation is impossible.' And likewise, it may be added, a psychological explanation would be impossible. The noumenal self, then, is itself unknowable, and yet somehow determines the whole course of the phenomena of one's moral life. Standing outside space and time (for to be within would involve being a phenomenon, an object of experience, and therefore a scientifically knowable thing), this self chooses this rather than that life. Kant holds that hereby he has reconciled science and morality (3.4). For the principle of causality has been saved in the sphere where it matters: while the concept of the noumenal self involves no self-contradiction.

3.37   Yet, subtle as Kant's approach may be, it contains the gravest difficulties. For first, the idea of a choice made in an individual human outside space and time is mysterious. And second, the choice brings something into being, for the choice made by the noumenal self must bring this life of mine into existence, rather than some other pattern of moral actions. Yet how can my moral life really be caused by this choice of my noumenal self? To suppose that it is means that again we have to apply the category of causality to the situation, and yet this is ruled out by Kant's own doctrine. We meet the same difficulty that we met above, in regard to things-in-themselves as underlying appearances (3.35). Further, Kant holds elsewhere that to count things involves time, the notion of succession (this, then that, then that). Thus to use either the singular or plural of something is only possible in the spatio-temporal context. How then can we talk of noumenal *selves*, in the plural? But if we do not we can't talk of individual responsibility (mine and yours and Henry's; here are three of us to start with). And without the idea of individual responsibility, there is no moral goodness or badness. The whole operation of saving morality will have broken down.

3.38 If then Kant's ingenious solution does not work out, what are we to say? What are we to say, that is, if we do not accept either physiological or psychological determinism (3.24, 3.34)? It is not enough that there should be random events, as we have seen (3.10); so a mere assertion that some human events are uncaused is in any event not enough, even if it were substantiated. What are the requirements of genuine freedom?

3.39 It must be that a free action is neither totally caused by what went before nor merely a random occurrence. This implies that it is an event which, given the preceding relevant conditions (the state of the organism and of its environment, together with the past history of the person, and the appropriate scientific laws, whether of physiology or psychology or both), could not be predicted with certainty. This 'could not' here means 'could not even in principle' (3.14), even if science were, so to say, perfected. By 'predicted with certainty' we mean something like this: an eclipse of the sun of a 1,000 years hence can be predicted with certainty. Or if some may jib at this, on the grounds that it is well within the bounds of possibility that there might be a solar catastrophe, say a stray star passing too close, let us narrow it down and say that an eclipse of tomorrow can be predicted with certainty, for we would know for certain that no stray star was in the offing and that all was well with the solar system. Thus what we are saying is that a free action must be unpredictable in the sense of not being predictable with certainty, even in principle, in a scientific Utopia. We now have to introduce a further condition, to save the action from being merely random.

3.40   There appear to be in general two ways in which novelty is not randomness. First, laws of nature may change. That is, it might be that laws are regularities which obtain only over a limited span of the universe's time. Of course, if this were so, we would doubtless wish to postulate a super-regularity, namely a law of change of laws of nature. Thus we would doubtless wish to avoid the suggestion that *all* laws of nature (so-called) were regularities that sooner or later would begin to fade. Nevertheless, it still might be true that, over a vast stretch of the universe's history, some regularities might change. However, this notion of non-random novelty scarcely helps us in regard to free will. The second way in which we could conceive of non-random novelty is this. It might be that some events are in principle unpredictable on the basis of past regularities, etc., and yet nevertheless have some kind of intelligible connexion with the events which precede them. Obviously everything here hinges on what is meant by 'intelligible connexion'. Let us try to give an example, by reference to the notion of *discovery*.

3.41   A scientific discovery seems to be something which is unpredictable in principle: for instance, Einstein's discovery of relativity theory. If it could be predicted (that is to say in reasonable detail) the discovery would already have been made. By definition, if you like, a discovery is unpredictable. It is true that, with technological developments especially, discoveries may in a very rough and general way be prophesied: but scarcely in detail. Imagine a super-physiologist who had full knowledge of the state of Einstein's brain before the discovery. Could he on the basis of that knowledge predict the discovery? Surely not, and for a number of reasons. First, even supposing that you could think of the brain as a kind of superb computer, the present state of the machine does not give the calculated results: for this you have to let the machine work. If indeed you could get future results out of the present state of a computer, it would be a marvel: a machine that can do its work without working. But then, letting Einstein's brain work involves his thinking, having an inspiration and so forth. To describe these matters, one has to go beyond physiology (as we have argued above).

3.42 But, it will be replied, this is hardly relevant: for though to get computer results you have to let the computer work, you could in theory (and most laboriously) work out its future state from its present one. Computers are determined, subject to the sway of natural laws. Likewise, Einstein may be so subject to laws, though they need not all be physiological ones.

3.43 True; but here we come to the second bar against the super-physiologist's success. A prediction about a discovery needs to be based upon a current scientific theory; but how can that theory already incorporate a new theoretical discovery to be made in the future? A scientific discovery, in transcending the present state of science, necessarily eludes current prediction. In the creative endeavour, men are forever getting one jump ahead of the contemporary situation.

3.44 Nor will it do to say that perhaps even so somebody in theory could have written down some equations and said that Einstein would formulate these. For unless the writing of them down meant that the predictor already had grasped relativity theory, it would just be a happy guess. Of course, anything can in theory be guessed; just as in theory monkeys using typewriters might hit upon the right words to compose *Hamlet*. But a guess is not a prediction, and shows nothing at all about the logic of events leading up to the result predicted. A woman sticking a pin into a football pool coupon may guess rightly: but her guess throws no light on what made Arsenal win. But the expert who *predicted* Arsenal's win would not just be guessing: he would know about the causes likely to bring that result about.

3.45 But even if it is granted that creative discoveries are in principle unpredictable, may this not merely indicate an inherent limitation in human knowledge, rather than an absence of causes? Underlying the events involved in a discovery, perhaps, there is at work a pattern of causes which is inaccessible to us. But to this,

we can answer that it is useless to speak of causes here if they are
inherently undiscoverable by us. Such determinism would involve
a leap of faith.

3.46 But because of this we do not want to describe such discoveries as random. They may be uncaused, or at least unpredictable
in principle, but they assuredly have an intelligible connexion with
previous science, and Einstein's illumination has a logical connexion
with his previous cogitations. We can call such connexions 'internal
connexions' to contract with the merely external relation that one
physical cause has to another, the 'looseness' and 'separateness'
which Hume spoke about (3.2). The novelty that occurs in the
Einstein case is creative, not merely a random event following upon
an otherwise orderly progression of causes and effects.

3.47 I have taken the case of scientific discovery: but similar
remarks might be made about other forms of creativity, in the arts,
for example. Here, there is still the intelligible connexion with a
tradition, and with an artist's training; but in creating something
new he transcends that tradition.

3.48 But, it may be objected, though all this is of great interest in
itself, what has it got to do with freedom in morality, which was
where we started? It may be that the genius like Einstein is in an
important sense unpredictable: but what about John Doe, who is
trying to do his humble best and live an honest and charitable life
in Surbiton? And, while we are on the subject, why prize unpre-
dictability so much? It's just because you can rely on John Doe,
that he is indeed predictable, that he's such a fine fellow.

3.49 But it should be remembered that John Doe's regularity of
behaviour (which indeed can be a good thing, if his habits are good
ones) is at least in part the product of training and of conscious
effort. People are not born honest, or willing to pay the tax-collector.
It is true that some people may have desires inborn in them which
make them more liable to break the moral law than others. But
nevertheless men's behaviour to a very great extent is artificial in
the sense that it is not a simple product of nature. People talk of

'nature's gentlemen', but the class is, I suspect, non-existent. In belief, the acquiring of the right sort of predictability is an achievement and, one is inclined to say, a human achievement.

3.50 But furthermore it must be stressed that no man is an island. The capacity to act morally or otherwise is in part due to men's rationality; and this in turn is due to the human power of language. But language is essentially a social phenomenon, so that in learning to speak and to think I am already borrowing a great deal from the rest of mankind. By consequence, just because I participate in a wider community, my actions cannot just be regarded as the result of an individual train of causes and effects within me and my immediate environment.

3.51 Let us return here for a moment to the Einstein example. If his discovery was in principle unpredictable, it follows equally that the fact that John Smith next door, who is studying physics and who has understood relativity theory, is exempt, too, from prediction. For how could we have predicted his understanding of an unpredictable theory? Similarly, if anywhere there are creative breakthroughs in moral insight, then there is a whole class of actions which are, in the relevant sense, uncaused. If Christ, for instance, has unpredictably taught something new, then men today are affected by something outside any rigid train of causes and effects. So creativity in moral insight, as its effects spread through the world, progressively liberates men from the determinism that would otherwise canalize their action and responses.

3.52 However, a difficulty crops up on the theological side. For it has been claimed that there are some creative moments in human life which are in principle unpredictable. But how could God, who is believed to be omniscient, fail to have foreknowledge of them? Do we have to say that God would not know how Einstein's cogitations were going to turn out? To save us from such a theological absurdity, we must specify a little more what we mean by 'predict' in the context of creative freedom. We must specify the basis upon which predictions can (or cannot) be made, and as follows. When I predict today what will happen tomorrow, it is upon the basis of knowledge of the present conditions of the situation in question, together with a knowledge of the appropriate scientific laws. This implies that prediction is a scientific operation, or at least, in regard to everyday, commonsense predictions, something which could be refined into a scientific operation. This would distinguish prediction from random guessing: anything can in principle be guessed, only one is very unlikely to guess right, and anyway a right guess tells us nothing about the causal antecedents of the situation which is foretold. The basis, then, of prediction is a pattern of initial conditions and causal regularities. And so, in saying that something is unpredictable in principle, we are saying that in some way it falls outside the regularities, so that on such a basis it could not be predicted. But this does not imply that God could not, on some other basis or in some other way, have foreknowledge of the event in question. It merely implies that God does not predict things. Hence the concept *foreknowledge* must differ from the concept *prediction*. And I suspect that, on theological grounds, we would be happy enough about the distinction. The picture of God settling down to work out when the next eclipse will be scarcely accords with our inner beliefs about him.

3.53 There is one further problem which must be looked at, as it will help us to see how far such an idea of creative freedom differs from Kant's attempted solution of the free will, and yet how also there is a likeness between the two. Though, we have argued, a free act is uncaused (it is not, that is, totally caused by that which precedes it), it nevertheless is an action *of* someone. We might feel tempted to say that after all there is a cause of it. *I* am the cause of it. Yet what am I except a succession of physical and mental states? And if the action occurred at 5.30 p.m. (zero hour for the action), then to say that I caused it may just mean that the succession of physical and mental states up to zero minus one second is the cause of the action. But this is ruled out by the hypothesis that the action is uncaused and creatively free. Does the action then not form part of me? Is it not part of the succession of events that we call me? Surely it must belong to me, or otherwise it is not my action, and if not my action then it is not my responsibility? And yet the whole point of freedom is that it is a presupposition of moral responsibility, obligation and so on.

3.54 Probably the key word in our perplexity is the word 'belong'. For we do not normally talk of my causing my actions (as though the 'I' is a cause lying behind the events we call actions); but rather of this action being *mine*. Of course, I do not possess my actions in the way in which I may possess a pair of trousers. Somebody can steal my trousers but he cannot steal my actions. I can give my clothes away, but not my deeds. Nevertheless, in a loose sense my actions 'belong' to me, for two reasons. First, by analogy with the case of the trousers, I am responsible for my actions. I must answer for them; for similarly I am responsible for my property: I must not leave it around to the possible detriment of others (I shouldn't leave my trousers on the highway). Second, my actions 'belong' to me because we also use the word in a colloquial way which is relevant to the present case. We talk of something 'belonging' to the same sequence, pattern, organization, etc., as something else: 'He and I belong to the same club'; 'This piece belongs to that jig-saw puzzle'; 'The two movements don't seem to belong to the same symphony' . . . and so on. Thus an action could be said to belong to a person in the sense of belonging to the same series as other activities of the person in question. That an action does thus 'belong' is manifest not merely from the fact that it is expressed in the behaviour of a certain physical organism; but also because it has an intelligible connexion with other actions and with a sequence of previous mental states. The same holds true of a creatively free action. There is thus no compelling need to assign to it a mysterious cause such as the 'self' (whatever this may be) or the person. Einstein the scientific discoverer cannot be dissociated from Einstein with the moustache; nor can relativity theory be divided from previous physics.

3.55 A corollary of this analysis is that the person is not constituted by a mere *causal* series of physical and mental states, but is open to novel and creative developments. The personality, then, is not just the result of a complicated interaction between various internal and external causal sequences; but is something which, to some degree, a person may create as he goes along. This idea is partly expressed in the Existentialist slogan that 'Existence comes before essence'. For this means that a person does not have a fixed essence or nature, so that life is a mere working out of the implications of it, through interplay with the environment. But rather action (or 'existence', i.e. acting existentially) determines one's nature. You make your character up as you go along. The person then is constituted by a sequence of events which is both causal and on occasion creative.

3.56 This conception of free will differs from Kant's, in that Kant asserts that only thought of as a noumenon is man free. He had to say this because he held that all phenomena fall under the principle that every event must have a cause. In short, all events, even human events, must have causes so far as they are observable. But the interpretation of free will as creative means denying that every event is strictly determined by prior causes. Both the idea of miracles and that of creative free will imply this rejection. Nevertheless the present interpretation has an analogy with Kant's doctrine, in two respects. First, creative freedom is like Kant's noumenal self, such that no strictly scientific account of it could be given. And second, just as Kant held that the moral law has a strongly rational quality, so that it is accessible to men's reason, so the idea of creative freedom, in holding that there must be an intelligible connexion between the action and what has gone before, implies that only rational beings could thus be free.

3.57 But it is important here to note what the connexion between free will and rationality entails. It can generally be seen that the capacity for thought and reflection, and thereby the capacity to create, depends upon the most remarkable of human institutions – language. But language is a social phenomenon: and it is not something which is, or could be, the private property of the lone individual. Hence, as we have seen earlier (3.50), a human being cannot realize his capacity for creatively free activities save in society. It is important to emphasize this, because too easily we tend, when moralizing, to think of freedom as something built into the individual, like his heart. This bears too on the myth of Adam; for as it is often rather literally interpreted, it suggests too individualistic an idea of freedom. Rather, we owe our freedom of will to our brothers, and no man is an island.

3.58 A further consequence of our picture of freedom as the capacity for creatively novel action is that free will in being connected with creativity in general is not simply to be confined to the area of moral activity. For again it is a defect of much thinking on this subject (and part of the fault lies with Kant for concentrating so much upon morality) that men's freedom is too much conceived simply as a presupposition of moral good and evil: as though we have a special organ, the will, which only comes into action when moral choices are being made. But this is to chop people up into different compartments, and is unrealistic. Rather, because men are capable of reflection, of self-awareness, of insight, of discovery, they are not, like moons and flatworms, constricted by the past, nor are they at the mercy of unconscious and uncontrollable causes. Freedom is as much in evidence in the choice of a picture for my room as in my rejection of a moral temptation.

3.59 This, too, is relevant to Kant's way of meeting the difficulties occasioned by Hume in regard to natural science. As we said (3.6) Kant claimed that the mind, as it were, supplied the order which characterizes the world considered as an intelligible object of scientific enquiry. This doctrine points to an important fact, namely that the concepts of science are not simply derived from sense-impressions. The empiricist account tends to picture knowledge as a passive consequence of the reception by us of sense-impressions. But a fruitful hypothesis is one which goes beyond the data it is meant to explain: and a rich concept is one which makes us see events in a new way. The human intellect here is creative and active, in its attempt to organize what is given in sense-experience. Here, then, we can appeal to human creativity in resolving Kant's problem, rather than saying that, somewhat mysteriously, the understanding, in its confrontation with the world, is supplied with a set of *a priori* concepts. What the mind has is initiative, not a set blue-print for constructing the world revealed by science.

3.60 To conclude, then, this essay stemming from a consideration of Kant's views on freedom, let us sum up the suggestions which have been made. We have argued that the attempt to reconcile freedom and determinism through the notion of juridical freedom (3.14) does not work, so that Kant's problem about reconciling science and morality (3.4) still remains. But we found difficulties in Kant's relegation of freedom to the noumenal self, which cannot be found in experience. At the same time we gave reasons for rejecting physiological determinism (3.32). On the basis of these dissatisfactions, we tried to outline a conception of freedom as creative which avoided saying either that a free act was determined by prior causes or that it was merely random. Both miracles and freedom were found to involve an infringement of the principle that every event must have a cause. Or rather, since in a sense both miracles and personal freedom fit into an intelligible framework, it would be better to say that they both infringe the principle that every event must fit into some pattern of observable regularities.

3.61 But it should be noted that we have not actually established that either miracles or creative freedom occur. We have merely shown how they are possible. We have tried to show that the conceptions of the miraculous and of free will can be given sense and consistency, despite the intellectual problems which they raise. But clearly there are no miracles, properly so-called, if God does not exist. And though there might well be freedom in an atheistic universe, the existence of God might be thought to strengthen in some measure the authority of the moral law: and this in turn would strengthen the conviction that what morality presupposes actually exists. Thus it is of the utmost importance that we should turn to consider the reasons and evidences for the existence of God.

4

Aquinas and God's Existence

4.1 IN turning to the proofs which have been offered of God's existence, we move both backward and forward in time from Kant. For the classical exposition of the traditional proofs was undertaken by St Thomas Aquinas, and he is, paradoxically, both a figure of the thirteenth century and a contemporary of our own. This is because the Encyclical of Pope Leo XIII (*Aeterni Patris*, 1879) urged Roman Catholic philosophers to draw their inspiration from St Thomas; and thus he is something like the 'official' philosopher of a great segment of Christendom. Though no human philosophy is a necessary condition of becoming a Catholic, nevertheless it is held that Thomism is the Christian philosophy *par excellence*. It is only with caution that the Roman Catholic philosopher should depart from the teachings of the Angelic Doctor, as St Thomas has been called. And it must be confessed on all sides that he is a very great philosopher, and his attempt to produce a synthesis of Aristotle and Christian doctrine is masterly.

4.2 The proofs are central to Aquinas' whole exposition of natural theology. For to have a natural knowledge of God implies that there is some sort of evidence in the world about us for thinking that a Being of such-and-such a character exists beyond the natural world. If there were no such evidence, our attempts to speak about God by comparison with what we know through the senses would come to nothing.

4.3 In the history of Western thought there have been three outstanding arguments for the existence of God, and of these Aquinas rejected one and formulated important versions of the other two. The three have been called the Ontological Argument, the Cosmological Argument and the Teleological Argument. The first argues from the essential nature of God to his existence ('ontological' literally means 'concerned with being'); the second argues that the cosmos must have a cause outside itself; the third argues from evidences of design or order in the cosmos to the existence of a designer or governor of the universe ('teleological' means literally 'concerned with purpose').

4.4 It was St Anselm (1033-1109) who gave the clearest and most influential version of the Ontological Argument, though other philosophers, notably Descartes, have also formulated it. Briefly the argument amounts to this. We define God as 'that than which no greater can be conceived'. We then suppose that God perchance does *not* exist. But we soon notice that this involves a contradiction, for an imaginary God, a God which we think about, but which does not exist in reality, is less perfect than a real God. For the imaginary being lacks one perfection, namely reality. It follows then that, if God is that than which no greater can be conceived, he must exist.

4.5 Both Aquinas and Kant rejected this argument, though for somewhat different reasons. Yet even rejection can be a compliment. For the power and simplicity of the argument have given it a great appeal; and no philosopher can make his position clear, one way or the other, without taking a stand in regard to this argument. There are two reasons why this is so. First, because it seems to present such a decisive proof of God's existence. Secondly, and more significantly, it contains in a nutshell the underlying principle of such metaphysical speculation. For it does not begin with observation of the world or seeing the way things are. It does not even start from an examination of experience or of the human condition. But purely *a priori* (3.6), and without reference to our experience of the world, it claims to show an enormous fact about reality. It enshrines in brief compass the principle that purely by taking thought one can add much to one's knowledge. No wonder that those who have an empiricist approach to philosophy, and who say that knowledge begins with sense-experience, are eager to show up the fallacies of this argument. If knowledge must begin with, or at least have a basis in, experience, then nothing like the Ontological Argument could bring knowledge.

4.6 Aquinas, whose philosophy has an empiricist strain partly derived from Aristotle, rejected the argument. His reasons were as follows. The argument begins with a definition of God; but this implies that we have an understanding of God's essence or real nature: a definition, in the tradition of Aristotle, reveals or makes plain the essence of the thing defined. If, for instance, I define man as a 'rational animal', then I am trying to show what man essentially is. But how can we pretend to have genuine knowledge of God's essence? Our apprehension of God through natural knowledge, by way of natural theology (1.12), must start with sense-experience. It is, therefore, indirect. Indeed, only God can apprehend his own essence. This is in line with much of the language of religion—for do we not say that God is incomprehensible, ineffable, unknowable? Not in the sense that he is totally unknowable and inexpressible, for then there could be no truths about him, no belief and hence no religious faith; but at least in the sense that God cannot be *totally* comprehended by us, even no doubt when he is seen (face to face). Aquinas does not deny that *if* we had a knowledge of God's essence we would see that his existence followed from it. But since we do not possess this knowledge, we are for ever precluded from using the Ontological Argument. The only person who could legitimately use it would be God: and to him it would, we can guess, be entirely superfluous. In any case, it is by no means clear that everyone understands by the word 'God' what Anselm wants him to mean. The pantheist (holding that in some sense the world is God) would no doubt challenge the definition. Further, it could only be in the case of God that existence and essence somehow coincide. In all ordinary cases, where we frame an idea, it does not follow at all that the thing represented by the idea exists. We have the idea of the unicorn for instance, but nowhere in the jungles of the world could you come across such a beast. Even if, then, we have the idea of a Being, in whom existence and essence coincide, it does not follow that such a Being actually exists.

4.7 Kant's criticism was perhaps more radical. For he would have had great difficulty in understanding or agreeing to Aquinas' view that the proposition 'God exists' would at least be self-evident to God. For if a proposition is self-evident, it is because it is true by definition, or as Kant would put it *analytic*. An analytic proposition is any proposition like 'All bachelors are unmarried' which is true because of the meanings of the words employed. It is part of the meaning of 'bachelor' that a bachelor is unmarried. Thus the meaning of the predicate ('unmarried') is included in that of the subject ('bachelors'). This is what Kant, and following him, many contemporary philosophers, would call an analytic proposition (judgment, statement, etc.) – as contrasted with those propositions where the predicate is not contained in the subject, such as 'All bachelors are melancholy'. These Kant called *synthetic* propositions or judgments (etc.). Now all statements about existence are synthetic, and a test of this is that they can be denied without self-contradiction. For obviously if a proposition were true by definition, one would run into a contradiction. Now we seem to have no difficulty about saying things like 'There are no electrons'; 'There is no such place as Agra'; 'Mr Khruschev does not really exist' and so on. All these propositions happen to be false; but they are not self-contradictory. We can conceive a world in which there are no electrons, no Agra, no Mr Khruschev. We can even for that matter conceive that there might have been no universe at all. It also seems to make sense to say 'There is no God'. The fool mentioned by the Psalmist may have been foolish, but not to the extent of contradicting himself. Thus the proposition 'God exists' is *not* analytic; and yet the Argument tries to make out that its truth follows from the definition of God. That is, it tries to make out that it *is* analytic.

4.8 All this can be seen by approaching the matter from another angle. When it is said, in the Argument, that if God did not exist he would lack a perfection, namely existence, this implies that existence is a kind of good quality. But can we really think of it as a quality? It is true that 'existent' is an adjective, and so grammatically is on a par with words like 'blue', 'powerful' and so on. But grammar can be misleading in matters of logic. To use Kant's example: what difference is there in quality between 100 imaginary dollars and

100 real ones? All the material and other qualities which we can ascribe to a real dollar can be ascribed, in our imagination of course, to an imaginary dollar.

4.9 If we say that something exists – say that lions exist – we are in the first word or phrase, 'lions', sketching out a blueprint of the kind of thing to look for (an animal having a mane, etc.), and we are asserting that something in reality corresponds to the blueprint. But if existence itself is a property, like having a mane, then it could be added to the blueprint. We could then ask: 'Do existing lions exist?' That is, does anything in reality correspond to the following blueprint: an animal having a mane, tawny skin, a big roar and the property of existing? But if it were meaningful to talk thus, it would be meaningful to say that some existing things do not exist. This is either a contradiction, or we are using 'exist' in two senses. Let us then invent a new word for the second sense, e.g. 'subsist'. But then is subsistence a quality? We get into the same trouble all over again, and so on *ad infinitum*. These, then, are some of the reasons why philosophers have adopted the slogan that existence is not a predicate. They have consequently rejected the Ontological Argument.

4.10 But the fact that God's existence cannot be self-evident does not, of course, imply that we cannot have good reasons for believing in his existence. These St Thomas Aquinas found in his famous Five Ways – five ways of arguing to the existence of God, starting from what is in the world and ending in the transcendent. The first three of these ways are different versions of the Cosmological Argument. They are, briefly, as follows. First, we observe that some things are in process of changing or moving. But if a thing changes its state or position, the change must be effected by some other thing which is already actually operative. But such an actual operation is itself an instance of change or motion. So the argument reapplies here again. But we cannot admit an infinite number of stages in this form of explanation, or we would never be in a position to explain the present changes taking place here and now. So there must be a first unchanged changer or unmoved mover. This Prime Mover is what everyone would recognize as God. The second argument is this. We observe that there are some efficient causes, that is, some things which bring other things into existence. But each efficient cause itself requires explanation in terms of some other efficient cause. By parity of reasoning with the first argument, there must be a First Cause. And this everyone would recognize as God. The third argument is as follows. Some things, we observe, come into existence and go out of existence. Thus they have the capacity either to be or not to be. But given an infinite time such a thing sooner or later would not exist. Thus if everything were capable of existing or not existing, sooner or later there would be nothing. If the universe then had existed from eternity there would be nothing now, since at some time in the past there would have been nothing, and nothing can come out of nothing. So not everything can be contingent (capable of existing or not existing). Suppose, too, that the universe had been finite in time, the same conclusion would follow. Maybe, though, the necessary or imperishable being which we must postulate to account for the existence of contingent things is merely hypothetically necessary. It is necessary if contingent beings are to exist. This still does not give us a final explanation (nor will it do to postulate a hierarchy of such necessary beings). We must therefore conclude that there must be an absolute necessary being, one which would exist whatever else did or did not exist. This Necessary Being everyone would recognize as God.

4.11   There is an important comment to make about these versions of the Cosmological Argument. They do not (as can be seen from the Third Way) involve arguing that the universe is finite in time. Aquinas is not saying that you can't have an infinite temporal sequence of causes going back in time. On his view, it could not be proved whether the universe was finite or not; and it was a matter of revealed rather than natural theology to believe that indeed the universe was created a finite time ago. What he is saying briefly is this: that to explain what we observe here and now we have to postulate a first Being who serves as the explanation. A system of explanation is a kind of hierarchy of principles; but no science can have an infinite number of increasingly general explanatory laws. There must be a first step.

4.12 An immediate query will be raised about Aquinas' claim
that everyone will understand by such phrases as 'First Cause',
'Prime Mover' and 'Necessary Being' – God. It would be odd for
me to say (on going to church), 'I am going to worship the Prime
Mover'. One still has to show that this Being has the properties
which we ordinarily ascribe to God. Of course Aquinas himself went
on from the Five Ways to deduce certain qualities which the Being
in question must have (such as goodness and so on) which do bring
it into line more with the common concept of a personal Object of
Worship. Nevertheless, the concept *God* as it is used in the Bible,
in worship and in doctrine is exceedingly rich. To understand what
it means (in the Christian context) one has to see how it functions
in a whole pattern of statements. A brief recapitulation of such
statements is to be found in the Creeds; and it is obvious that the
concept is much richer than the somewhat austere notion of First
Cause, etc. Or, to put the matter in another way, how are we to
show that the God of metaphysics corresponds to the God of
personal experience? All this may be a cause of some dissatisfac-
tion with such arguments for God's existence: they may show
something, but they do not show us the God of Abraham. The
enormous conclusion which we wish to arrive at is bigger than the
premisses will allow. Perhaps it's like Crusoe trying to deduce the
real Man Friday, with his individual character, from his footprint.
We shall return to this point later. But in the meantime, let us be
fair to Aquinas. Having made the distinction between those things
which can be known through natural processes of observation and
reasoning from those things which have to be revealed, it would
obviously be absurd to expect him to produce arguments in natural
theology which conclude with the revealed God of Abraham. All
he has to show is that the metaphysical God is sufficiently like the
revealed God for us to accept that both in fact are identical.

4.13 Kant had two main objections to the Cosmological Argument.
It should be noted that the actual version he criticized was one which
he took over from his philosophical predecessors in Germany, and
which corresponded most closely to the Third Way. The first objection – one which is echoed by many contemporary philosophers –
is that the Argument, in employing the idea of a Necessary Being, is

secretly smuggling in the error already detected in the Ontological Argument. For to describe God as a Necessary Being is tantamount to asserting that the statement 'God exists' is necessarily true. But we have already seen that it is not self-contradictory to deny statements about existence, and you could only make 'God exists' necessarily true by making existence part of the definition of God – a move which involves, in effect, the use of the Ontological Argument. But, as we shall see (4.27ff.), the Cosmological Argument can be stated in a form which is not open to this objection.

4.14 The second criticism turns on the correct use of the idea of a cause. As we saw, Kant argued (3.7) that, for a proper scientific understanding of the world, it is necessary both to use concepts like *cause* and to apply them to experience. To try to use such an idea to apply to something which lies beyond all possible experience lands us in contradictions. Now the Cosmological Argument attempts to show that there is a First Cause lying beyond all the particular events which go to make up the cosmos. It therefore must, according to Kant, lie beyond all possible experience. Hence the Cosmological Argument cannot yield any scientific knowledge. Kant does, it is true, hold that the idea of a First Cause has a certain use in guiding scientific enquiry, since it expresses the notion that science progresses towards an ideal limit. That is, we can quite legitimately frame the idea of a First Cause as an imaginary target for science to aim at in its continuing investigation of the chain of causes and effects in the world. But it is a target which in the nature of the case can never be reached. It is like the end of the rainbow which for ever draws us onward, though we would be foolish to expect to get to where the coloured arc touches the ground. Thus the Cosmological Argument brings us the idea of a First Cause; but such a Being cannot be thought of as real, but only as a useful piece of science fiction.

4.15 Both these objections are important and illuminating. The first raises a fundamental question about a deep-rooted feeling which we may have. For it is natural, when one is in contemplative mood, and viewing reality in all its strangeness, to conceive that there might have been nothing, instead of what there is. Why does anything exist at all? Here we are afflicted with a sense of the contingency of things, of their possible non-existence. It is partly by enshrining this sense of contingency that the Cosmological Argument gains its power over us. But nevertheless, when we have asked, 'Why does anything exist at all?' what answer are we to expect? If we are going to postulate the existence of some Being which will explain why there is something rather than nothing, then it is no good just postulating a contingent Being – one which possibly might not have existed. One would have to bring in the idea of a Being which exists necessarily, which could not *not* exist. But then we have already seen, in Kant's first objection (4.13), why the idea of such a Being is invalid.

4.16 Nevertheless, the question, 'Why does anything exist at all?' retains its rather peculiar fascination. It cannot so easily be dispelled: and we still feel that it is trying to say something. The reason perhaps is that though it is too generally and abstractly expressed, we want to ask something of more limited scope. For initially what we want to know is not why *anything* should exist, but why the universe, the *cosmos* should exist. We are not so much asking about everything that is (for God, too, is covered by this phrase), but about the cosmos in which we find ourselves. This is the first lesson which can be learnt from Kant's objections.

4.17 The second objection (4.14) can be further clarified by recasting the Argument in terms of the cosmos, and as follows:

(a) Something exists, e.g. this tree;
(b) To explain the existence of a thing, it is necessary to show that it occurs in a network of causal relationships: for instance, this tree came into being from a seed, and the seed . . . and so on;
(c) But any such network belongs in a wider network, namely the cosmos;
(d) It is conceivable that the cosmos might not have existed;
(e) So we want an explanation of the existence of the cosmos;
(f) But we cannot place the cosmos in a network of spatio-temporal causal relationships, for such a network is by definition part of the cosmos;

(g) Hence the existence of the cosmos would have to be explained by reference to a transcendent cause – that is, one which is not in space and time, and somehow lies 'beyond' the cosmos.

4.18 Now it is quite clear where the trouble lies. The second step says that an explanation of why something exists involves showing the network of causes (in space and time) in which that thing occurs. But the last stages show that such an explanation, in terms of a being in space and time, could not possibly be forthcoming in regard to the cosmos as a whole. Is not then the idea of such an explanation self-contradictory? This is a similar point to the one which Kant is making. In brief, it means that we begin the Argument by appealing to causal relationships which science can establish: but we end up in a region beyond all possible science. For science deals with things and events which are observable, and which occur in space and time. Yet in attempting to argue ourselves beyond the cosmos we seem to be going beyond the observable, and outside space and time.

4.19 This provides us with another lesson—namely that any attempted explanation of the existence of the cosmos is non-scientific. It is worth stressing this point, for two reasons. First, it implies that the theist has to reject the view that all knowledge is, in principle, scientific. Partly in order to introduce simplicity into their account of the world, and partly because of the amazing successes of scientific enquiry, philosophers have been tempted to claim that there can be no matters of fact which cannot in principle be established by observation. Such a view lay behind the Verification Principle which formed the linch-pin of Logical Positivism, and which affirmed that the meaning of a statement lies in its method of verification. This implied that statements which could not be verified by sense-experience are meaningless. For instance, if I say, 'There is an invisible, intangible, etc., fairy in this room', my utterance comes to nothing, for there is no way of showing it to be either true or false. If anyone, sceptically, were to complain, 'But I can't see it or smell it' and so on, I might answer, 'But it's not that sort of fairy: didn't you hear me say that it couldn't be observed in any way?' Such an unverifiable assertion is meaningless or vacuous. So far, we may feel quite sympathetic to the Principle. Still, it has grave, and perhaps unacceptable, consequences. For likewise if anyone speaks of God as Creator of the cosmos, the Principle will condemn him for uttering the meaningless. As we have just seen, in postulating such a transcendent Cause of the cosmos we have to go beyond the observable. Thus as far as *observation* goes, and as far as science goes, there can be no way of verifying the claim. But then, do we want to be put into the Positivists' straitjacket? As we have noted earlier (2.42), people certainly claim some kind of awareness of God, even if this is not a matter of observation in the ordinary sense. Moreover, there is no reason in the nature of things, so far as we can tell, why there should not be different types or kinds of knowledge. But we shall return to this point later. Suffice it for the present to note that if the Cosmological Argument is to work at all, it must involve a non-scientific explanation of the existence of the cosmos.

4.20 The second reason why it is useful to insist on the non-scientific character of the doctrine of the creation is that too often Christians are inclined to hail discoveries in cosmology as 'proofs' that the world was created. For instance, in recent times there has been some dispute between those astronomers who have propounded the theory of continuous creation and others holding alternative views, e.g. that the universe started with a 'big bang'. The former theory, by postulating that hydrogen atoms very occasionally come into existence out of nothing, but in sufficient quantities to keep up a supply of new galaxies, implies that the universe is in a steady state, i.e. it must look, taken in large enough doses, the same from any point and at any time. This in turn implies that it is of infinite duration. Now, recently, the radio-astronomical researches of Professor Martin Ryle appeared to supply evidence *against* this theory; and a London evening paper saw in this a 'proof' that the Bible is right. (Perhaps the journalists forgot that the Bible, if taken literally, has got its dates very wrong, and where is the big bang?) Yet as we saw, the Cosmological Argument, if valid, is quite compatible with the eternity of the cosmos. In any event, it is always open to the scientist to hold that there was something before the big bang, or that a revision of his highly speculative theory is preferable to the introduction of an extra-scientific concept, namely God, into his account.

4.21 So far, then, we have concluded, as a result of Kant's objections, that if we want an explanation of the existence of the cosmos, it must be non-scientific. But we have to consider two further objections which arise out of this conclusion. First, why should there be an explanation for everything, for are not some states of affairs just inexplicable? And second, is it in any case legitimate to talk about the cosmos in the way we have been doing, as though it is a single thing?

4.22 Regarding the first of these difficulties, there is a seemingly powerful answer. For where a state of affairs is contingent, it always seems appropriate to ask why this state of affairs rather than some other exists. Even absurd contingent statements, such as 'The moon is not made of green cheese', represent states of affairs which can be explained. If the moon *were* made of green cheese, it would disintegrate! Indeed, is it not our normal hope that any given state of affairs can be explained? Still, it will be replied that we have already argued that (3.8) it was not self-contradictory to hold that there could be random events. And are not some sub-atomic events – admittedly within well-defined limits – random? And what kind of explanation of the random can be given?

4.23 But the well-defined limits are important. So far as we know, the random occurs within the general framework of regularities. In general, contingent events, etc., can be explained; this remark can be dubbed the Explanatory Principle, which is a weaker, yet more flexible, version of the principle that every event must have a cause (3.8). There is no good reason to abandon the Principle just because we allow the theoretical possibility of random events and because we concede that there is an element of randomness, within well-defined limits, in a certain class of phenomena. Moreover, belief in the miraculous, as we saw, involves belief that certain events are *scientifically* inexplicable, but in the very description of them as 'miracles' we are proffering a type of explanation (that God caused the events).

4.24 But what of the other difficulty? It may well be thought that we cannot sensibly talk about the cosmos as a whole. The term 'cosmos', the objection would run, is only shorthand for the open class (2.25) of events which are in principle observable or which can be given locations in space and time. But a class is not the same as a member of the class; certain questions which we can legitimately ask about members cannot meaningfully be asked about the class. For instance, we can ask, 'When was that tiger born?', but we cannot ask 'When was the class of tigers born?' – as though the race of tigers, like the individual tiger, must have a parent.

4.25 Nevertheless, the concept of a cosmos or universe is commonly used in scientific cosmology, and implicit in it is the assumption that all events are related in a single framework. It does not seem absurd to think of the cosmos as a vast pattern of events, and as such it can be thought of as a single entity, just as a table, which is a pattern of events, is thought of as a single thing. Admittedly, the question why this vast pattern exists has a different flavour from the question why any particular event within the pattern occurs: for, in the latter case, the question can be answered by tracing out the causal ancestry of the event; while, in the former case, the only explanation available is of a quite different sort. Still, if we can speak of the cosmos as a vast pattern, and if this pattern might not have existed, it is not absurd to seek for some account at a different level which will make its existence intelligible.

4.26 Yes, but what kind of account? All that we seem entitled to say so far is that the cosmos might not have existed, and that by applying the Explanatory Principle (4.23) we can legitimately hope that there is an explanation for its existence. We can argue that somehow 'beyond' or 'behind' the cosmos there exists a Being which explains the existence of the cosmos. Let us call it the 'Cosmos-Explaining-Being', or 'CEB' for short. But what profit is it to say this? The CEB is a bare idea, and nothing is said about the way in which it brings the cosmos into existence. It is a mere empty hypothesis. And again, the CEB might not have existed; it needs explaining too.

4.27 As regards this latter point, what we must remember is that the object of an explanation is to produce a gain in intelligibility. To postulate a further Being beyond the CEB will not, I suspect, help in this direction. It is true that some Greek and Indian theologians have conceived of a hierarchy of Beings transcending the cosmos, the one emanating from the other. But there have usually been rather special, religious reasons (see below, 5.47) for doing so. These we shall come to anon. But meanwhile we can perhaps simply content ourselves with speaking of a CEB, without delving into the mysteries of what (if anything) lies beyond. Entities are not to be multiplied beyond necessity. But then (it will be objected), wouldn't it be simpler still to forget about the CEB, and just say that the cosmos explains its own existence? Or in Aquinas' terms, why shouldn't the cosmos itself be the Necessary Being? Sooner or later, it seems, we have to arrive at something which is self-explanatory. This is perhaps just another way of saying that you do not have to look outside the cosmos for any explanation of its existence.

4.28 But something vital follows from all this. To be important the notion of a CEB must be enriched. One would have to show what such a Being would be like and why it is plausible to hold that the existence of such a Being explains the existence of the cosmos. Otherwise the explanation ('The cosmos exists because of the CEB') will be as stupidly empty as saying 'I'll tell you why I have a pimple on my chin: it is because something caused it.' But what caused it? And how? These are the substantial questions. Yet how could the Cosmological Argument ever tell us about the what and how? If the only two data are: first, that the cosmos is contingent; and, second, that everything contingent needs explanation; then how could we ever get beyond such vacuous empty notions as First Cause or CEB?

4.29 Our trouble is that we are too much inclined to look upon such metaphysical arguments as though they must be deductive (2.14). We think of them as analogous to syllogisms such as this:

> All Chinese smoke opium;
> All Cantonese are Chinese;
> Therefore all Cantonese smoke opium.

There is a real sense here in which the conclusion is contained in the two premises. In drawing the conclusion, we are not going beyond anything contained in the premises. But it is wrong to model all our intellectual activities on this pattern. As we saw, creative science involves a leap (3.59); a good explanation transcends the data which it is meant to explain. Even in simple generalizations this is so. I see a tiger, and it is tawny; and then another, and it is tawny: so I conclude that tigers are tawny. If, then, and by contrast, we stick to thinking of the Cosmological Argument as purely deductive, we shall end up with merely barren conclusions. For the conclusions drawn will only be contained in the rather bare premises. To appreciate the Argument rightly, we must take a new view of it, and see it as posing a problem, namely that the cosmos is contingent. This problem can only be solved illuminatingly by making an imaginative leap, and proffering an explanation which is much richer than that of a bare CEB.

4.30 It has already been argued that in speaking of the CEB as cause of the cosmos we are going beyond scientific explanations. But how can we do this? How can we have the idea of a cause which does not fit into a scientific theory? Fortunately, we have already framed such an idea. We sketched out an account of creative novelty in human actions which does not fit completely into the pattern of regular causes and effects (3.56). Now, admittedly, this creative novelty exists in the setting of a network of causes. But could we not more boldly conceive of an act of will or discovery which has no such context? – pure creativity, as it were? It would be analogous to a human act of will, because of its creativity: but it would be different, because it has no spatio-temporal setting.

4.31 Such a notion might be thought mysterious; but it does not seem to be self-contradictory. Moreover, the idea of pure creativity involves the concept of creation out of nothing (since no causal conditions underlie it or confine it); and this concept in turn can to some extent be understood by reference to analogies which we use in other contexts. For example, a striking and original work of art brings into the world something new: it is not just a rearrangement of elements already used by others (though it may actually include this). It is not surprising that the word 'creativity' is used here: for it would be misleading to think of the artist as having built something up out of what was already given. In an important sense, he has made something from nothing.

4.32 Let us then hazard the claim that the explanation of the existence of the cosmos is due to an act of pure creativity. This has the merit of introducing an analogy with the human will; and yet at the same time of using an idea of cause which is different from that employed in the physical sciences. It thus fulfils two important conditions. First of all, it is in some degree intelligible. Second, it means that the CEB is of a different type from the physical cosmos, so that the explanation is not a scientific one. For, as we saw (4.19), such an explanation of the existence of the cosmos must of necessity be non-scientific. On the other hand, if we had spuriously tried to erect a scientific explanation of the cosmos – for instance, by thinking of the CEB as a kind of colossal dollop of electricity – then we would only have thereby voted the CEB into the cosmos. But, of necessity, the CEB must transcend the cosmos.

4.33 All this enables us to reformulate the Cosmological Argument in the following way. We see that particular things exist, and find that the explanation of this drives us to form the idea of a vast network of causal relationships in space and time. This great pattern forms the cosmos. But we see that it is conceivable that the cosmos might not exist; and by appealing to the Explanatory Principle, we seek to know why it does exist. We also see that any explanation must go beyond the physical sciences. In this state of perplexity, we jump to the conclusion that the cosmos comes into being through an act of pure creativity. In short, the Cosmological Argument poses a problem; and we have suggested an answer to the problem.

4.34 But it is worth repeating that not everyone will admit that there is a problem. For (the sceptics will say) we should follow Kant, and affirm that since the proposed explanation of the cosmos is, necessarily, non-scientific, it is an improper explanation. And a problem which does not admit of a proper answer is an illusory or unreal problem. It is like the question, 'Which direction does a flame go when it goes out?' Yet although people may wish to dissolve the problem in this fashion, they must recognize that they can only do so by insisting that facts must be of a certain sort – capable of confirmation through scientific enquiry. Once this doctrine is questioned, the problem posed by the Cosmological Argument must reassert itself. For if there can be extra-scientific facts, facts about a transcendent Being, for example, then there can be an extra-scientific explanation of sorts for the existence of the cosmos.

4.35 However, our proposed solution to the cosmological problem may meet with rather a different objection. Though we have enriched the idea of the CEB by describing its operation in terms of an act of pure creativity, having some analogy to human creativity, this hardly helps much, for it still remains a very thin and abstract idea. Admittedly, 'purely creative act' is an advance on 'cosmos-explaining being', but even so, how detailed is the idea? But this objection is premature. Not only might it seem reasonable to say that a Being which is creative must also possess something like consciousness, but it may turn out that there are good reasons for identifying the creative CEB with God. In this case, the explanation of the existence of the cosmos which we have suggested would be linked up with a whole lot of other things, with religious experience, with historical events and so on. In any event, the idea that the world is created by an act of will – almost arbitrarily, we feel – chimes in with that sense of radical contingency which afflicts us when we contemplate the possibility that there might indeed have been no world.

4.36 By itself, then, our version of the Cosmological Argument leads us to a rather tenuous, but meaningful, hypothesis. It is because men believe that the Will who created the cosmos is in some measure accessible to human experience that the hypothesis acquires a deep and important significance. Thus natural theology cannot stand alone, but must examine the reports of revelations and disclosures of the Transcendent in human experience. This need to go on to revelation does not mean that the Argument is unimportant. For it already gives us a reason for believing in a transcendent Being of a personal nature. It perhaps does not provide a very *strong* ground, just by itself. But it is an indispensable part of any belief that the God who discloses himself in human experience is also the source from which the cosmos flows.

4.37 The philosopher, then, has to go on eventually to examine revelation and religious experience; but we shall reserve the discussion of this till later. It is enough here to point out that Kant, in taking it for granted that the First Cause lies beyond all possible experience, ruled out the validity of revelatory experience. For him, science and morality exhausted the avenues of knowledge: there was no 'third' way, the way of religion as such. Not surprisingly, then, in his *Critique of Practical Reason* he made religious beliefs essentially depend upon morality. The ultimate consequence of this way of rescuing religion is to destroy those central values on which religion depends – the value of worship, for example. But whether or not men have seen God, at least some have claimed to do so. It is not absurd or impossible that some of these experiences may reflect the nature of the Being who, if our version of the Cosmological Argument has any force, brought or continually brings the cosmos into existence. At least any philosopher of religion ought to investigate this claim. In the next chapter we shall go into this vital question. In the meantime, let us turn to the Teleological Argument, a version of which was formulated by Aquinas in his Fifth Way.

4.38 We observe, he argues, that many material, and therefore non-intelligent, things of different kinds co-operate in producing a stable world-order and stable sub-systems. They thus achieve an end or purpose. But being material they cannot consciously bring about this end. So the situation implies the existence of an intelligent Author of nature who guides things in such a way that they achieve this end.

4.39 It will be seen that Aquinas here appeals to a highly general example of purposiveness. It is the fact that the cosmos is stable and 'works' in a regular and co-operative way. Other philosophers and theologians who have argued to an intelligent Author of nature on the grounds of apparent design in the universe have looked to a particular class of examples, for instance, that the bodily organs of animals such as the eye appear to be designed, so cunningly are they

contrived and so well-adapted to the animals' needs. It is therefore clearer if, in the following discussion, we distinguish between
the examples, calling the one 'cosmic orderliness', and the other
class 'biological adaptation'. Thus Aquinas stresses cosmic orderliness, while Paley, for instance, in the latter part of the eighteenth
century, emphasized biological adaptation.

4.40 Now obviously, if we accept orthodox Evolutionary Theory,
we can picture the way in which biological adaptation has arisen
without appealing to the notion of an intelligent Author of nature.
For the apparent cunning with which organs and environments are
adapted to each other is due, on the Theory, to the interplay of
natural selection and genetic variation. A shuffling of genes, inter-
spersed with some mutations, and a vast proliferation of lives and
deaths are enough to do the trick. Thus there is quite strong scientific
evidence, only available since the time of Hume and Kant, for being
suspicious of the simple appeal to biological adaptation as showing
the existence of God. On the other hand, interestingly enough, Evolutionary Theory makes us see biological adaptation as a particular
instance of cosmic orderliness – that species, like galaxies, evolve
through the interplay of regularities. Thus Evolutionary Theory cuts
at the root of the special, but not of the general, form of the Teleological Argument.

4.41 Hume, in his posthumously published *Dialogues on Natural
Religion*, subjected the Argument to a detailed scrutiny and criticism.
The main points which he made were as follows. First, the Argument involves comparing the whole universe to a human artifact. It
is the similarity between the regular and co-ordinated operation of
the cosmos and the contrivances of human art and technology which
forms the basis for inferring that there is an Author of nature who
bears some resemblance to human beings. The cosmos goes like
clockwork: and clocks are made by intelligent beings. But, says
Hume, why single out human artifacts? If we are comparing the
whole cosmos to a small section of the items contained in it, that is,
comparing the whole to a part, why not select some other part?
For instance, the cosmos seems as much like a vegetable as it is like
a machine. But if we make the comparison in this way there will be

no need to infer an intelligent Author. Potatoes are not, in our experience, designed by men.

4.42 Second, even if we accept the machine comparison, there is no need to think that there is only one Author. A savage on first seeing a ship might infer that a wonderful and powerful craftsman must have made it. But a person who knows that, though a single person can make a canoe, it takes a host of craftsmen and designers to produce the Queen Mary, will make quite a different inference. It might equally be, then, that the cosmos was designed and co-ordinated by a committee of gods, rather than by one God.

4.43 Third, the theist is in a dilemma. For the stronger the Argument, the more blasphemous is its conclusion. The strength of the Argument depends on the closeness of the similarity between a human artifact and the cosmos. Like effects have like causes: and the liker the effects, then the liker the causes. That is to say, the liker the cosmos is to a machine, the liker is the Author of nature to the designer of a machine. But it would be blasphemous to think of God as very like a human. So, if the Argument were very strong, it would be theologically unacceptable; and if it were theologically acceptable, it would have to be rather weak.

4.44 Fourth, Hume touches on a difficulty which is universally recognized – the existence of evil and disorder. If the orderliness of the cosmos is evidenced by an Author of nature, evil and dis-orderliness must be counted as counter-evidence.

4.45 Finally, it is convenient, too, to mention a criticism thought of by Kant. It is similar to the second objection described earlier (4.14) which he levelled at the Cosmological Argument, namely that even if we observe a chain of means and ends in nature, it is wrong to think that this indefinitely extended chain could ever be experi-enced in all its completeness. In short, the Being which is postulated as the ultimate cause of the chain lies beyond all possible experi-ence: and such a Being can never enter into a system of theoretical or scientific knowledge.

4.46 Hume's first difficulty (4.41) depends essentially on two main points: first, that, as a matter of fact, the cosmos is as like a vegetable as it is like a machine; and second, that, regarding the inherent orderliness of a plant and of the cosmos as a whole, there is no *a priori* reason why inherent orderliness should not be characteristic of things. Why should it be surprising that things are orderly? Would it be less surprising if they were chaotic? In regard to the first point, the situation is odder than at first sight appears. For the features of the cosmos and of the machine which are being compared are so highly general – for they are supposed to be alike in respect of stability and co-ordination – that any sub-system within the cosmos, such as a plant, will fit the comparison equally well. That is, both the cosmos and the sub-system contained in it will resemble each other in respect of orderliness as much as either resembles a machine in this respect.

4.47 This point can become clearer by considering in more detail what we mean by a machine. A machine has three relevant characteristics. First, it is a complex of interacting parts. For this reason, we feel disinclined to call a pen a machine: it is too static and simple; but a typewriter we do call a machine. Second, a machine's operation has a specific effect or function. A harvester harvests, a clock tells the time and so on. For this reason, we feel disinclined to call a sculptor's mobile a machine: it does not have a use outside of itself. Third, a machine is designed and produced by human beings to fulfil the said function. For this reason, though we use horses for riding and ploughing, we do not call them machines, for they are produced by nature, not strictly by us, even if we breed them. In what respects, then, can the cosmos be compared to a machine? First, the cosmos could be regarded as a complex whole made up of interacting parts. Second, this interaction, though it does not have an effect outside of itself, nevertheless results in a kind of consistency and stability within the system (and so it is really more like a mobile). But can we infer from these resemblances that the cosmos has a Designer and Producer? No doubt some people are tempted to say 'Yes' just because machines are complex things whose origins we understand clearly, whereas even a plant's mode of coming into existence is to some degree mysterious. Still, there are cases where it is not too hard to describe ways in which a complex whole comes into existence out of a more chaotic state: for instance, we can sketch out various theories to an account for the origin of the solar system. It is true, however, that in order to elaborate such theories it is necessary to include reference to existing regularities, that is to say, to the functioning of laws of nature. The emergence of the organized out of the relatively chaotic implies that even the relatively chaotic is not *completely* chaos. In short, to explain orderliness, we must presuppose some degree of orderliness. And here we meet a situation just like that which we encountered in discussing the Cosmological Argument. For we cannot explain the origin of the ordered cosmos *as a whole* in terms of a prior orderliness, a prior pattern of events governed by regularities. For again, by definition, such a pattern would itself be part of the cosmos (4.32). Once again we are faced with a choice. Either we say that there can be no explanation of the orderliness of the cosmos *or* we can say that the only explanation would be non-scientific and not in terms of causal regularities.

4.48   Reference back to the Cosmological Argument is important here. For it will be remembered that there it was vital to frame the idea of the cosmos as a whole, since the problem posed by that Argument is that there might have been no such cosmos. The reason why it may be so regarded as a whole is that it is constituted by a vast pattern of interacting events in space-time. Thus the Teleological Argument, by drawing our attention to the orderliness of the cosmos, and its resemblance to a machine just in this respect, reinforces the claim that we can think of the cosmos as a single whole. It repeats what we already need to know in order to work the Cosmological Argument.

4.49   But what then does the Teleological Argument add to the Cosmological? The latter involved our conceiving that there might have been no cosmos. What similar conception does the Teleological Argument involve? Surely, in drawing attention to the orderliness of the cosmos, it involves our conceiving that the cosmos might have been quite disorderly. For instance, it might have consisted of an enormous quantity of atoms buzzing about in a random way. Yet even such a universe would be organized a bit: for if there were no stability or regularity whatsoever, how could we single out individual atoms? True disorderliness – absolute disorderliness – would be utter chaos; but here we could no longer speak of this, that or the next thing. In effect there would be no cosmos. Nothingness and absolute chaos would be indistinguishable. It is therefore part of the conditions for the existence of a spatio-temporal thing that there should be some degree of orderliness. The Teleological Argument, then, has to begin with more than the fact of orderliness if it wishes to infer an intelligent Author of nature. It must show that the degree of orderliness unmistakably shows that the cosmos must have an intelligent Cause.

4.50 But we have already seen that the cosmos could as well be compared to a sub-system as to a machine. Thus the Argument cannot establish that we must infer a Designer. Consequently, we must concede Hume's first objection (4.41) (though this means that we need say no more about his third (4.43): if we are abandoning the argument that like effects must have like causes we need not worry at the dilemma which it creates).

4.51 But even so, the Teleological Argument poses some important questions. For instance, it cannot be supposed that whatever the laws of nature were, conscious life would be bound to evolve. The universe of buzzing atoms which we imagined would not bring forth the complexity required for sentient existence as we know it in the cosmos. Hence, there is something about the degree of orderliness in the actual cosmos which poses a problem. We may ask: 'Why this highly organized cosmos, rather than another sort?' The answer cannot be given (as we have seen (4.30)) in scientific terms. But we argued, in the context of the Cosmological Argument, that Kant's straitjacket needs to be rejected. Thus again, we can repeat the point in the face of his objection to the Teleological Argument (4.45). Of course our explanation of the comparative orderliness of the cosmos means going beyond science. But you have to do that once you admit the possibility of a transcendent being.

4.52 It is true that the disorderliness and evil of the world must be taken into account too. Hume is quite right (4.44) to cite it as counter-evidence. But the problem of evil is too big to be dealt with just now: and it will be reserved for a later discussion.

4.53 We see, then, that the Teleological Argument, like the Cosmological, poses a problem. Why should there be a cosmos containing so much orderliness? Why indeed should it be sufficiently orderly to give rise to conscious and rational life? Again, we must make a bold leap, and try to sketch out the beginning of an answer. It is as follows.

4.54 It is hard to see what value could be attached to a dead universe, one which was bereft of consciousness. It is true that God might for some mysterious reason create it, perhaps as a kind of toy. But leaving aside such queer guesses, let us contemplate a blind swirling of atoms and galaxies. It would go about its unconscious business; but there would be no value or virtue in it. There would be no enjoyment, no creativity, no struggles and successes. No, for the cosmos to produce value, it must first produce conscious beings.

4.55 It is not surprising that Kant, for all his scepticism about the Argument, should have remained deeply impressed by 'the starry heavens above and the moral law within'. It is not just that the stars, jumbled though they are, are regulated by scientific laws. More than this, they call forth awe and a recognition of their serene majesty. We can appreciate their beauty: they are a marvellous instance of the glories of the natural world. And yet a world composed only of stars, or only of unconscious atoms, would have no beauty. This is not to say that beauty is in the eye of the beholder: but it is nothing without the eye of the beholder. In recognizing the glory of the stars and the call of the moral law, we recognize that the universe contains that which is valuable: and we are prepared for the question: 'Why this sort of cosmos?' Now if we accept the explanation which was hazarded as a result of the problem posed by the Cosmological Argument, that is, if we believe that the cosmos is brought into being by an act of pure creativity, then it may be not at all unreasonable to answer the problem posed by the Teleological Argument as follows: a cosmos orderly enough to produce consciousness and values must have been produced by a Being who prizes these things. This is to say that the purely creative CEB prizes goodness, beauty, creativity. In some way analogously to human beings the Creator is a source of values and in some way he is good.

4.56 This solution is relevant to the Fourth Way of Aquinas. This argument, less celebrated than the four great proofs which we have been discussing, is, briefly, as follows. We notice among things different degrees of perfection: things are good in varying degrees. This scale of value implies a supreme limit, i.e. a being which is supremely perfect. (Good and better imply the best possible.) Now since lesser degrees of anything are caused by the supreme degree of that property – all heat being caused by fire, the limiting case (so Aquinas thought) of heat – then the supremely perfect being is the cause of the less perfect beings. On Aquinas' view, moreover, all existing things have some degree of perfection, however small, so that the supremely perfect being is the cause of everything else. This Being we understand to be God.

4.57 Certainly today the Argument from Degrees of Perfection must be regarded, as it stands, as invalid. For, first, we do not need to think that because there are more or less perfect instances of a thing there must be a supremely perfect instance. May is a better cricketer, so we may think, than Oakman. But this does not imply that (laid up in heaven as it were) there is a supremely perfect batsman (even Bradman falls short of this ideal! – not that we can have a very clear notion of what an instance of that ideal would be like). Second, the principle that the extreme instance of something causes lesser instances is clearly false. Heat can be produced by friction rather than flames, and in any event the middle of an H-bomb explosion is hotter than ordinary fire. Nevertheless, a somewhat similar argument, but in different form, is sometimes used in the attempt to show that objective values (e.g. moral values) require an objective 'source', and this source is identified with God. It is argued that if values are objective, they do not proceed from the subjective desires and choices of human beings. But whence do they come, then? It cannot be said that, say, the moral law arises from material causes. If then it proceeds neither from the material world nor from the world of conscious beings, it must have a source beyond the world, i.e. a transcendent Being.

4.58 There is a good deal of ambiguity in such an argument. For the words 'objective' and 'subjective' are notoriously unclear. In saying that something is objective, we may mean one of two things (at least): either, first, that the thing exists independently of human beings, or second, that there are public ways of deciding the truth (etc.) about the things in question. For the first sense we shall use the word 'objective', and for the second sense we shall use the word 'intersubjective'. Thus the moon is objective; and the statement, 'That house is beautiful' is intersubjective (for arguments about the question are not a mere matter of personal taste). Now certainly the moral law is intersubjective, for we can reasonably argue about points of morals. There are criteria of truth, and so on. But what meaning could be attached to saying that the moral law is objective? How can we say that it *exists* independently of human beings? After all, the statement, 'It is wrong to steal' is not a *thing*, like an apple-tree. In talking of the moral law as objective we would be imagining it as a kind of mysterious and invisible substance pervading we know not where. And once on this slippery slope of thing-making, we would slide further, much further. Would we not have to count the truths of mathematics as things existing independently of human beings? And so on. There would be a world of ideas, like those of Plato's theory, existing independently of the world of experience. Abstractions would be made concrete.

4.59 The trouble arises in trying to treat the moral law as a kind of thing. It is better English, and much less confusing philosophically, if we simply consider it as a set of rules or statements. And about these the important question is not. How did they arise? – but rather: Are they true, and for what reasons? We can of course ask how they arose, and the answer involves going into the history of morals. But we should be more interested in whether they are intersubjectively true. In any event, the attempt to argue that there must be a source of objective values rests on the confusion between rules and things.

4.60 Further, as has often been pointed out, moral laws cannot be deduced simply from statements of fact. As Hume said, you cannot get an 'ought' simply from an 'is'. For instance, it does not follow from the fact that adultery causes the break-up of marriages that adultery is wrong. We require further the judgment that it is *wrong* to break up marriages. This is not of course to say that 'is' statements are irrelevant to moral questions. Indeed they are highly relevant, and a lot of stupid moral judgments are made because of ignorance of the facts. But it still remains true that without notions like *ought* or *wrong* or *valuable* occurring somewhere in the premisses, you cannot deduce a conclusion containing such notions. Now this point means that we cannot simply rest morality upon some metaphysical fact. We cannot justify the moral law by saying simply 'It proceeds from God', for we need the further *moral* judgment that we *ought to obey God*. Thus there is an important sense in which moral judgments are autonomous, and the moral law must stand on its own footing. Hence, it helps little to try to show that the moral law has a 'source' from which it proceeds. It is this recognition that leads Kant to postulate God on the basis of the moral law and not the other way round.

4.61 But have we not ourselves been trying to say that God is a source of values (4.55)? If the Moral Argument rests upon a confusion and a naïveté, then how can this notion of a 'source of values' be defended? Let us be clear about it. What we were arguing before is that values are not objective, though they are intersubjective. They are not objective, for if there were no conscious beings it is hard to see how there could be any application for concepts like virtue, beauty, and so forth. Of course we could say that moral laws would hold hypothetically, in the sense that in a humanless cosmos adultery would still be wrong (meaning: Suppose there were human beings, it would be wrong for them to commit adultery). Values would, so to say, potentially, but not actually, exist. That is, valuable states of affairs would be there potentially, rather like the valuable diamond mines that might perchance exist on Alpha Centauri. (But what value are they to anyone?) Thus, for things to become actually valuable, conscious beings must exist and enter into relation with them. But further, we find that conscious beings themselves (as being capable of creativity, virtue and so on, and as being capable of personal relationships) are themselves valuable – indeed they are the beings, within the cosmos, which have the highest value, so far as we know. It is, then, as the source of valuable things and beings that we can speak of God as the source of values.

4.62 But, the sceptic may say, why should not valuable things arise out of the unvaluable? The seed of a flower by itself may be worthless, but the flower which proceeds from it may be a lovely thing. Likewise out of the jungle-law of long ages of evolution, from the squirming amoebae and from the dull diplodocus, man has emerged – something of value out of the relatively valueless, something wondrous out of the dull and dreary. Why not? We often witness the transformation thus (as the Marxists put it) of quantity into quality.

4.63 The objection is fair enough, except that it misses the main point. If the Cosmological Argument poses a problem and if we solve that problem by postulating the creation of the cosmos by an act of pure creativity; and if, given this explanation, we add that the cosmos might have been much more chaotic than it in fact is, and that by consequence it contains life, consciousness and values, which it might not have done; and if then, on the basis of the Cosmological Argument as we have propounded it, we claim that the creative will has produced orderliness of such a degree as to create valuable things – is it not then reasonable to assert that this cosmos was chosen by the creative will because the latter prizes the valuable? It is not denied that the valuable empirically may arise from the valueless. Thus far the sceptic is quite correct. But given the notion of the creative will, we are perhaps entitled to infer, from the relatively ordered nature of the cosmos, that the creative will, as being the ultimate source of good things and persons, itself cherishes value – is itself in some sense good, by analogy with human beings: one of our main reasons for prizing humans is that they can create order and beauty where it before scarcely existed. To choose the valuable is itself a sign of value. So, since the creative will (according to our explanation) chooses a relatively ordered and creative world, this is a sign of the goodness of that transcendent Being.

4.64 We see, then, that the main force of the Moral Argument is not that without introducing the notion of God one cannot make sense of morals (notoriously one can); nor does its force lie in the thought that if moral values are 'objective' they must have a 'source' which somehow brought them into being. Rather it lies in the fact that consciousness and creativity are a necessary condition of there being actually valuable things and persons in the cosmos, and that the cosmos needs to be relatively ordered for there to be an emergence of consciousness and creativity. The thought that the cosmos might well have been less ordered, together with the thought that an explanation of the existence of the cosmos is that it was brought into being by an act of creative will, lead us to suppose that the transcendent Being prizes the valuable, and is thus (by analogy) in some sense good.

4.65 Some, however, may feel a grave difficulty in this account. The difficulty is that in our previous arguments about creativity it was claimed that creative acts cannot be predicted on the basis of a knowledge of causal regularities (3.60). In short, the creative act is something which does not follow simply from past conditions. And yet now we are picturing the cosmos as if God sets it in motion in such a way that consciousness and creativity will emerge. But, it will be said, if creativity does not simply result from past conditions, neither can the capacity for creativity. In short, there is no way of setting up a causal process (say evolution) which will ensure that the end product will have the capacity to act creatively. How then is the orderliness of the cosmos a guarantee that there will be valuable things?

4.66 The first thing to say to this is that what we previously argued was that a degree of orderliness is *necessary* to consciousness and creativity. A guarantee, on the other hand, is a *sufficient* condition of something (a necessary condition is such that if not it (A), then not the result (B): a sufficient condition, by contrast, is such that if A, then B). So the fact that a causal process would not be sufficient to produce consciousness, etc., does not destroy our previous argument, since we only held that a high degree of orderliness was necessary to it.

4.67 Nevertheless, to leave the matter there might seem most unsatisfactory. For we are presented with the picture possibly of God's setting up the evolutionary process, without ensuring that it would have the desired result. Somehow the emergence of the capacity to act creatively would be beyond his control. And this appears strange and improbable. We have, of course, been assuming too blithely that the premiss that the capacity to act creatively cannot be the result of prior causes is true. Need this be accepted? But, whatever our answer to this question, the fact that the capacity to act creatively does not follow as a result of prior causes does not entail that the emergence of it was beyond God's control. For God chooses just this cosmos, knowing in advance (so to speak, for he knows all at once) that creativity will in fact emerge amid the necessary regular patterns of cause and effect: or, to put the matter another way, he is the Continuous Creator.

4.68 There is a final main objection to the way in which we have argued which will have to be considered. It is this. We have said that though the Teleological Argument is in itself invalid, it does nevertheless draw attention to the fact that the cosmos is less chaotic than it might have been, and this fact is highly significant in virtue of the fact that through this complexity life and consciousness and creativity have emerged. It might be commented, by way of objection, that if we are going to say that one particular fact about the cosmos (its containing consciousness) is to be explained by reference to the existence of a transcendent Being who prizes values, then any particular fact will have some kind of similar explanation. But this means that theological explanations will everywhere compete with scientific ones. Once we are on this slippery slope, we are bound to end in swamping science with theology. Hence there must be a radical defect in the line of approach. For we *know* that we can give scientific explanations which are perfectly adequate in themselves. It is therefore absurd to come along with another lot on the ground that 'ultimately' scientific explanation is inadequate. If we are to say, 'Strange that the cosmos contains life: we must seek a metaphysical explanation of this', why not also say, 'Strange that that man has a wart on his nose; there must be a metaphysical explanation of it: why should the universe be such that it contains such a phenomenon?''?

4.69 First (in answer to this), the explanation which we have proposed (4.55) emphatically does not conflict with any particular scientific explanations. The latter can perhaps account for the origins of life, etc., in terms of existing patterns of regularity among inanimate objects, and so on. The transcendent explanation in no way supersedes these accounts. It in no way conflicts with them. It merely asks (when all the explaining has been done) why there are such regularities as there are, and gives an answer in terms of a transcendent Being. It is, it must be repeated, encouraged to do so because of the explanation suggested by the Cosmological Argument.

4.70 Second, it is perfectly true that if the Supreme Being has chosen just this cosmos out of all possible ones, then even the tiniest fragment of it (the hairs of a man's head, the sparrows) is chosen by God. Every event, however tiny, must fit into a pattern that is essentially good. But to say this in no way destroys the idea of scientific explanation.

4.71 Third, it happens that the existence of persons, of creative beings, is (so far as we can judge) the single most significant feature of the cosmos. It is moreover not just a tiny feature (like the number of hairs on my head). The astonishment we may feel that there is a cosmos at all (4.16) is paralleled by the astonishment we may feel that there are persons, conscious beings. There might not have been. To think of them away (and oneself away) is a far, far bigger item than thinking the moon or the galaxy away. One might expect then that an inkling of the point of purpose of the cosmos might be found here, in this vital feature of it.

4.72 But of course some may think that we are being too man-centred, too anthropocentric. Conscious beings may be just a flea-bite on the vast face of this truly enormous and staggering cosmos. Why should we try (despite Copernicus and Einstein) to put ourselves back in the middle of the picture? Pride, pride – that was always our trouble.

4.73 But it is not necessarily being man-centred and proud to think that conscious beings who can act creatively are the most valuable things in the cosmos. Perhaps elsewhere amid the teeming stars a similar race exists: they too would display the same value. It is not just bias or prejudice to claim that consciousness, with its adjuncts of knowledge, enjoyment and creativity, adds a new dimension to the cosmos. A new category is born. Moreover, if there are no actual values without consciousness, and if the idea of significance includes that of importance, which is itself a value concept, then assuredly there must be a special significance in the birth of consciousness. Indeed, the rise of rational beings must be overwhelmingly significant. And in any event, what is our possible bias contrasted with? With the dispassionate pursuit of truth? But there can be no such pursuit of truth without the existence of conscious and rational beings.

4.74 We can now sum up the results of this essay upon Aquinas' Five Ways. We have seen that the Cosmological Argument, though not *deductively* fruitful as some in past times have thought, nevertheless poses a problem. It poses one, that is, provided that we are ready to go beyond the limit which Kant and Logical Positivism have set, and to concede that there can be a non-scientific kind of explanation of the existence of the cosmos. The problem is that the cosmos might not have existed; and so the Argument impels us to look for an explanation of why in fact it does. But the explanation must use some idea other than that of a physical cause. Already, however, we have seen that human creativity goes beyond physical explanations, and so some analogy to this suggests itself as a possible account of the way the cosmos comes into existence. Admittedly, this means making a leap beyond the evidence: but we have to do this anyway, in science and elsewhere, if we are going to produce fruitful and illuminating hypotheses. Our analogy with human creativity is not, of course, perfect, for human creativity depends upon certain necessary conditions. Only if a man's heart is functioning can he act at all. So, then, the act of creativity which brings the cosmos into existence must be unconditional, an act of pure creativity.

4.75 We went on to examine the Teleological Argument, both in regard to cosmic orderliness and biological adaptation. The latter fact is helpless now to show anything directly about an Author of nature, because of Evolutionary Theory, though it does increase our faith in cosmic orderliness. But though the argument is open, even in its general form, to very serious objections, it does draw attention to the fact that the cosmos is more orderly than it might have been. In particular, it has that degree of orderliness required for the evolution of conscious and rational life. Given the idea of pure creativity as a result of contemplating the Cosmological Argument, we can perhaps hazard the additional (and again non-scientific) explanation that the transcendent Cause created this type of orderly cosmos because it cherishes values. The only force of the Argument from Degrees of Perfection and of the Moral Argument is exactly this.

4.76 It will be seen that our whole argument depends on certain key ideas. First, that of uncaused creativity (3.60); second, the notion of the cosmos as a single whole (4.25). Clustering about the first idea are others, like that of consciousness. The importance of these to our argument is that they help to provide the grounds for rejecting physiological materialism. This in turn is vital: for it is necessary to see that not all events can in fact be given an explanation in terms of physical causes. Without some distinction between the consciously creative and the physical, we would have no material at our disposal to frame an explanation of the existence of the cosmos which went beyond the physical sciences. Thus the investigation of the nature of personal existence is not only of great importance in philosophy generally: it is central, too, to the philosophy of religion.

4.77 But important though it may be to see that we can have grounds of revelation for belief in a Creator, it would be rather barren to confine ourselves simply to natural theology. Does the CEB reveal himself more intimately to human beings? Indeed, we criticized Kant (4.37) for not properly allowing that we might conceivably have experience of the transcendent Cause of the cosmos. We might be tempted at this point simply to fall back on revelation, and say that, having sketched out an area of belief which can be derived just from contemplating the cosmos about us, we must go to revelation for further details about God's nature and acts.

4.78 Yet how do we locate this revelation? Over a large period of European history, of course, there has only been one live option as far as revealed scriptures go. Revelation meant just the Bible. But with the opening up of the world, and with the scholarly investigation of the great Eastern religions, other scriptures have to be taken into account. In examining the nature of the experience of the Transcendent and of scriptural authority, we must go beyond our own tradition. If Christianity be true, it must surely be capable of giving reasons, and not simply rely upon a dogmatic appeal to the Bible. In any event, anyone, Mormon or Buddhist or Muslim, can make a similar appeal. But which tradition is the true one?

4.79 It is Rudolf Otto's greatness that he tried not only to repair the omission in Kant's philosophy by examining the nature of specifically *religious* experience, but also he broke away from the narrow confines of European culture and drew upon our new knowledge of the great religions of the East. For it is parochial and unphilosophical just to identify religion with Christianity. To be fair, we must examine the claims of other great faiths, and the insights gained in long and noble traditions that lie outside Christendom.

5

Rudolf Otto and Religious Experience

5.1 RUDOLF OTTO represents an important trend in modern philosophy which is largely absent from the thought of the people that we have been discussing. Whereas Aquinas, Hume and Kant tend to take religious ideals for granted, and to argue about the existence or otherwise of God and so forth, Otto attempts to give an analysis of religious thought and experience. He tries to unfold the characteristic nature of religion, as distinguished from other aspects of human life. Though he was brought up in the Kantian tradition, his new analysis of religion was bound to lead to very different results from those obtained by Kant. Moreover, his work steadily drove him to look widely at manifestations of religion throughout the world, particularly in the East. In this Otto gives us a salutary lesson that philosophy needs to be backed by knowledge in some detail of the facts of human existence: and it is quite clear that 'human existence' does not just include European existence. Too often people talk about the condition of modern man, and think only of Europe and America, forgetting that rather different ways and conditions of life are to be found in Asia and Africa.

5.2 Otto was also well aware that Christian theology, though it includes an intellectual element, is not simply an intellectual exercise. He was therefore concerned to reform and revitalize the ritual of his own Lutheran Church. In a chapel not far from Marburg he tried to develop new forms of devotion and worship, and thereby had a considerable influence upon the liturgical thinking of his fellow-Christians. He was also much concerned with missionary activity, though he was unfavourably disposed to the narrowness of many missionary attitudes. In fact, it may generally be said that a knowledge of the profounder side of Eastern religions tends to drive one away from the simple evangelistic approach which so many missionaries adopt. Further, of course, the sectarian differences between Christians become increasingly meaningless the further one is away from Western society and culture, and so it is not surprising that Otto, too, should have been much concerned with promoting Christian unity. He thus had considerable influence in the spheres of philosophy, theology, the comparative study of religions, liturgy, mission work and the ecumenical movement – a breadth of impact rarely to be found in this modern, rather specialized world.

5.3 Otto was brought up in the Kantian tradition. But he saw the inadequacy of Kant's description of experience, which led Kant into the position of basing religion upon morality. And he wished to establish that just as Kant had argued for the autonomy of morals, i.e. the thesis that morality is based upon an independent principle, the Categorical Imperative, and thus is not a form of science, so likewise religious knowledge is autonomous. According to Otto religion springs from a certain kind of experience, which he called the 'numinous' experience – the word being derived from the Latin *numen* meaning the divinity or power implicit in a sacred place or object. And just as Kant had elaborated a system of categories (3.6) such as causality, with which we 'make sense of' the world of experience, so Otto posits the category of *the holy* as that which unifies what is given in numinous experience. This apprehension in experience of the holy is the primary datum in religion, and theological ideas are secondary to it.

5.4 He analysed the numinous experience in terms of the Latin phrase *mysterium tremendum et fascinans*: what is apprehended is a mystery which is awe-inspiring and fascinating. A mystery, because the object of religious experience is basically non-rational: we cannot entirely think through and clarify it by means of ordinary concepts – hence many of the troubles which beset the theologian. It is awe-inspiring or terrifying, striking us into a state of dumb wonder – as many reports of religious experience indicate. But at the same time it is fascinating. Though a man, when confronted with the Holy, thinks of it as Wholly Other – there is so to speak a great gulf fixed between sinful man and the holy deity which he confronts – nevertheless he is drawn towards it. He is drawn towards holiness, and despite everything, towards salvation, for salvation is nothing other than the sharing in the holiness of the object of man's worship.

5.5 The non-rational apprehension of something transcendent, according to Otto, is then expressed through various symbols or 'ideograms' as he calls them, ranging from the primitive symbolism contained in the idea of the Wholly Other, through mythological representations, to the formulations of theology. His insistence on the 'non-rational' element is connected, for Otto, with the idea of autonomy of religious experience and thought. The sense of the holy or sacred does not yield knowledge about the empirical cosmos; it does not yield the kind of knowledge which we gain in scientific inquiry. Neither, on the other hand, is it simply an apprehension of a moral command. But dimly and dumbly it points towards the Transcendent. Thus Otto goes beyond Kant in postulating a third range of experience and knowledge: beyond scientific understanding and the moral law there lies the *a priori* (3.6) category of the Holy. Such in brief is his philosophical teaching, though it must be remembered that one of the chief merits of Otto's great work is the wealth of illustration from the history of religions by which he illuminates what he means by the numinous experience. One of the most striking of these many illustrations is from the Book of Genesis, and I mention it to show how Otto is drawing our attention to the living examples of religion which provide the chief justification of his analysis of the Holy. 'Behold now,' said Abraham, 'I have taken upon me to speak unto the Lord, which am but dust and ashes.' Otto comments that in this and other such examples you find the feeling of 'impotence and general nothingness as against overpowering might; dust and ashes as against "majesty"'. Unless we look to genuine examples of this sort which show the impact of religion in terms of experience and feeling, we shall fail to understand the heart of religion. A merely intellectual inquiry into ideas like Prime Mover or Necessary Being is not enough if it cannot be linked up with the living streams of religious experience. It is Otto's achievement that he has brought philosophers back to trying to describe and analyse the essentials of religious experience. For this reason, my brief account of Otto's position is scarcely adequate: the reader would be well advised to read through *The Idea of the Holy* to see the flesh in which the bare bones are encased.

5.6 We see that Otto clothes his account of the holy in Kant's terminology. Perhaps it would be useful to rid it of this clothing, and try to state his position in more ordinary words. First, he is claiming that there is a range of experience, namely that which he dubs 'numinous', which is of a special kind and which was ignored by Kant. Second, the key idea which unifies this range of experience is *the holy*. But third, the right application of this idea results in objective statements (or rather, to use our own terminology (4.58), intersubjective ones). These are central to religious language. God, that is, is essentially a *holy* being. Fourth, these statements contain a 'non-rational' element. This means that, first they are not simply theoretical or scientific assertions or indeed moral ones – i.e. statements about God or gods cannot be *reduced* to these latter kinds; second there is something inexpressible about the nature of the Being or beings referred to in these statements. Let us examine these claims.

5.7 First, let us draw out certain implications of Otto's analysis of the numinous as involving the recognition of a *mysterium tremendum et fascinans*. One can see from the excellent examples which he gives that the sense of the terrifying mystery of the divine implies a converse sense of one's own inadequacy and lack of holiness. Not for nothing does Otto speak of the 'otherness' of the divine. It follows that a consequence, as it were, of the experience is the sense of separation of men from God. And we note that when the numinous is expressed through systems of theology, the notion of a duality between God and man is insisted on. It is blasphemous for men to identify themselves with the Holy Being. The right reaction towards the holy is worship, and it is blasphemous and absurd for the worshipper to identify himself with the Object of worship.

5.8 Otto has certainly illuminated an important type of religious experience. But perhaps he has not adequately represented the nature of mysticism – that is, the quest, through contemplation, for inner insight and peace. Here the example of Theravada Buddhism, which flourishes in Ceylon, Burma and parts of South-East Asia, is absolutely crucial. For in this form of religion, which goes back to the Buddha's original teachings, there is no belief in a creator God, and the central teaching concerns nirvana, a transcendent state which it is possible for saintly men to reach. In doing so, they must not merely display moral goodness of the highest order, but must have become capable of profound spiritual contemplation. In this, Buddhist mysticism has similarities to the mysticism of the West. But it must again be emphasized that it is mysticism without belief in God. And though the Buddha did not deny the existence in the universe of gods, they are ultimately of little importance; and the Buddha himself, though superior to the gods because of his inner enlightenment, is not an object of worship. The peasant who lays flowers before an image of the Buddha in a temple is, strictly speaking, only paying homage to the memory of the supreme Teacher, now departed. Thus the sentiments of awe before a holy Being, and the sense of the fearful otherness of the Deity, have no place in the Theravada. In brief, though in the ordinary religion of these Buddhist countries there are numinous elements, the central affirmations of this faith do not at all concern the numinous object of worship which plays so important a part in religion elsewhere. Hence, though Otto's analysis is extremely important, and illuminates a great area of religious experience and practice, it does not really cater successfully for mysticism.

5.9 But this fact is obscured by a further important feature of religious history. Although, as we see from the example of Buddhism, it is possible to have a form of mysticism which does not at all involve interpreting the mystical experience in terms of union with God, and so on, nevertheless this kind of interpretation is not uncommon in the history of religions. The mystic who is nurtured within a theistic faith, for instance, naturally so interprets his profound inner experience. He thinks of himself as attaining a foretaste at least of the beautific vision of God which the faithful can expect in heaven. Consider too the religion of the Upanishads. Here the final revelation is that the eternal self, the Atman, which the individual can discover, so to speak, within himself through mystical contemplation, is identical with the sacred reality, or Brahman, which sustains the cosmos. In brief, the numinous and mystical strands of experience and language are here brought together in a single unifying doctrine. But though the fact that the two strands are so often woven together gives some plausibility to Otto's claim that the numinous is central everywhere in religion, we should not forget that they can exist independently of one another. Although often worship and mysticism go together, they do not always do so.

5.10 In line with this account, we can give a brief and crude account of phases in the life of the great religions. Thus in the Old Testament and in early Islam, for instance, the sense of the numinous exists in the most intense way, but the mystical quest is absent. On the other hand, in early Buddhism, in the Theravada and in Jainism the mystical quest is central, and there is little place for the religion of the numinous. But in the Upanishads, and in varying ways in most of Hindu history, there is a blend between the two kinds of faith; and likewise Islam flowered, through the Sufi movement, into a religion incorporating both elements: just as also we find mysticism in Christianity. Ironically, Buddhism in its development and spread changed its character. In the form of the faith known as the Mahayana, Buddhas became objects of worship and expressions of a transcendent reality lying behind the cosmos; moreover in the more extreme sects in the Mahayana one can find the doctrine that salvation comes through calling on the name of the Buddha in faith. This has obvious similarities to the insistence in Christianity – and particularly in Protestantism – that salvation comes through the grace of God, and not through the efforts of men. Here a numinous religion of worship has developed from what in origin had no place for this strand of experience.

5.11 Needless to say, this extremely brief survey of the great religions is a drastic over-simplification, but it may help to illustrate the account of religious experience which has been offered. Yet the account may cause uneasiness. For (it may be said) is it not unsatisfactory that we cannot single out some one item common to all religious experience? If at the heart of every faith there were some single insight or intuition, it would make it easier to believe that religious experience yields knowledge. If every great teacher in essence taught the same thing, would we not be surer that religion contains truth? These questions, of course, bear upon the whole harrowing problem of whether we have to make a choice between religions, and how this rationally can be done.

5.12 Two different points need to be disentangled here. First, an old-fashioned (and Aristotelian) view of definition suggests that if we use the same word of various things then all these things must have an essential element in common. But there is no need to be spell-bound by this view of how words work. In many cases we use the same word of various things not in virtue of their having a common nature, but in virtue of the fact that the things possess a family resemblance. The game of patience has its likenesses to rummy, rummy to whist, whist to a foursome at golf, golf to hockey, hockey to football, football to baseball, baseball to cricket. But tell me: what have patience and cricket got in common, barring some punning relationship? The same, I suggest, is true of the great religions. They have a complex pattern of family resemblance, but there is no need to start off with the assumption that there will be some essential, central, common element.

5.13 Second, it might be true that if all teachers agreed, we would be surer about the essence of religious truth. But in the nature of the case, we must distinguish between experience and interpretation. And the interpretation of an experience depends in some degree upon the religious environment and the doctrinal context within which the teacher or seer works and lives. We would thus not expect a detailed agreement. It would be absurd to suppose that all the details of the creeds could be 'seen' to be true in a single religious experience. The notion of such close agreement, then, is at bottom unrealistic.

5.14 Nevertheless, the fact of family resemblance does introduce some degree of unity into the picture. There are certain, admittedly rather looser, similarities between the prophetic and contemplative experiences which we have distinguished. Indeed if it were not so how would it be thought in some phases of religion that it is plausible to think of the mystical experience as being in some way an experience of God? And, though the central content of the Buddhist mystic's experience on the one hand and that of Muhammad's prophetic experience on the other hand differ greatly, there is in both the sense of a transcendent being or state, as though somehow here both had an insight into what lay, so to speak, beyond space and time. There are other loose similarities to which we can point, but I mention this one as being central to our theme. For we wish to find out if experience of the transcendent can be shown to be valid.

5.15 To return, however, to Otto. The fourth element in Otto's position mentioned above (5.6), namely that the central aspects of religious language cannot be reduced to scientific or moral language is clearly right. It is one of the faults of Kant's exposition of religion that in essence he reduces it to morality. It is true of course that the great religions contain profound ethical teachings, and one of the remarkable features of the Old Testament prophets lies in their welding together of the insights of religion and morality. But though true religion may *include* morality it does not simply *consist* in it. The two great commandments of Jesus illustrate this point very clearly, for though loving one's neighbour is central to morality in this life, loving God goes beyond our worldly ideas of morality. Morality is primarily concerned with human relations, religion goes beyond this. Moreover, as Otto points out in his analysis of the holy, the terrifying and mysterious aspects of divinity are experienced independently of beliefs about the moral goodness or otherwise of the object of worship. For this reason, the teaching of the prophets, that God's holiness includes the demand upon men of moral goodness, represents a real discovery.

5.16 Again, the attempt to reduce religious faith to belief in a number of metaphysical propositions about the ground of the cosmos and so on must always seem unsatisfactory, for inasmuch as God is a Being whom it is appropriate to worship, and who manifests himself in awe-inspiring experiences, he is not simply to be equated with the conclusion of a metaphysical inference. This does not imply, of course, that the metaphysical beliefs are themselves unnecessary if religious belief is to be belief about reality. But it does imply that there must be reasons for identifying the metaphysical God with the God of religious experience and practice (4.12).

5.17 Further, we discover, and no one has illustrated this better than Otto, that religious experience has its own kind of inner logic. The holy Being, for instance, is the source of grace in virtue of its being both terrifying and fascinating. For men cannot without blasphemy presume to become God: but at the same time they feel drawn towards that which is holy. Thus they hope for holiness but realize that there is only one properly holy Being, or, in short, their hope of salvation lies in a portion, so to speak, of the divine holiness being transferred to themselves. In such ways one can observe patterns of thought and practice arising out of the numinous experience. We might put all this in another way by saying that the pattern of religious language has its own peculiar and special structure, just as other areas of language, e.g. morals, aesthetics, and so on, possess their own characteristic forms of inference. So, then, we have good reason to accept Otto's thesis that religious language cannot simply be reduced to other forms of discourse. It follows that an important task for the philosopher is the analysis of this area of discourse. For this purpose the investigation of different religions can indeed be illuminating. One can discern thereby the typical features of religious thinking.

5.18 Now if this claim is correct it could throw some light on the second point of Otto's described above (5.6). If religious thinking is, so to speak, autonomous or independent (5.3), then we may find within it some guides as to how religious truth is to be arrived at. Of course it is clear that we shall not find any absolutely knockdown arguments which would persuade any perceptive and pious person of the truth of one set of beliefs rather than others. For since perceptive and pious persons can be found in different religions and denominations, such arguments would have to have the effect of converting them. But we see from experience that it is comparatively rare for people to change their faith. But this need not destroy the validity of the point we are making. For certainly we can discover tests of the truth of religion which would at least be recognized as relevant by adherents of other faiths. The fact that men argue about religion indicates this. And though we are not in a position to produce knock-down arguments, the arguments and considerations themselves may have a long-term effect, may weigh as time goes on in a social rather than a personal dialogue. Likewise, in discussing literature or art, we find that relevant points though they may not individually seem decisive have in the long run their appropriate effect. Further, in religion, just because in its higher forms it deals with the spirit rather than letter, we should not expect an absolutely cut-and-dried solution to central problems. This does not mean, however, that we should not try to be as clear and as consistent as possible. These are virtues by any reckoning. But on the other hand we should not be unduly depressed that there cannot be 'proofs' in any rigid or absolutely persuasive sense (4.36).

5.19 Still, though it is important to describe the internal logic of religious language, and though this will yield insights about the tests of religious truth which we shall attempt later on to describe, nevertheless the existence of internal criteria may not be a guarantee that there is truth to be found in religion. For consider witchcraft as a parallel. Within the realm of magical language one may discern characteristic patterns of reasoning. Given that there are witches there may be tests which would lead one to identify particular persons as witches. Likewise, there may be broad principles which are appealed to to explain the peculiar ways in which witchcraft functions effectively. But all this does not entail that there is any truth in witchcraft. Educated people reject witchcraft, even as a possibility. Its power has faded from the scientific mind. It no longer seems much good as a form of technology or medicine. Its basis and assumptions have been rightly replaced by more rational and empirical ones. So then, we feel, witchcraft as a doctrine contains no truth, even though there is an internal logic within the language of magic. The whole way of speaking and thinking has to be scrapped. Likewise, some may affirm that the whole way of talking, thinking and acting religiously ought to be scrapped, for it has no basis in reality. Or in more concrete terms it may be held that religious experience cannot give us any knowledge of reality: it is not a valid means of knowledge. This indeed is the central problem of the philosophy of religion.

5.20 But before going on to discuss it, it may be well to resist an objection that may be raised. It may be felt that the central fount of religious knowledge is revelation rather than religious experience. Is it not by God's revelation that we are guided and controlled in our beliefs? Should we not then be discussing the notion of the validity of revelation rather than of religious experience? And yet how can we discuss the former, for if truth comes from God in revelation, then human reason is not adequate to pass judgment on it?

5.21 We should, however, be clear as to the nature of revelation. We have had occasion to note (2.2) that revelation is God's self-disclosure rather than the mysterious descent from heaven of a string of propositions. But God does not disclose himself in a vacuum. To disclose oneself one has to make oneself apparent. To make oneself apparent is to make oneself apparent *to* persons or peoples. Leaving the miraculous aside, though it ought to be regarded as a special form of self-disclosure on the part of God, revelation must surely take the form of a kind of personal encounter or vision. Think of the inaugural visions of Jeremiah and Isaiah or what happened to St Paul on the Damascus Road. Once we dig behind the written documents of the scriptures we discover that at the heart of revelation there lies religious experience. Thus there is no split between the two enquiries: the one into the validity of religious experience, the other into the validity of revelation.

5.22 And yet is human reason capable of judging these visions? Yet what does the question amount to? Does it mean that the content of the visions is not the result of a process of thinking? If so, then all right. Who would expect there to be a substitute for experience when it comes to discovering the nature of reality as it actually is? We cannot arrive at truth about reality simply on the basis of thoughts and calculations (4.5). But if the question implies that we can have no reasons for recognizing something as a revelation, then it must be rejected. But since reasons for the recognition of a genuine revelation are part of the internal logic (5.17) of religious discourse, can we judge as to whether any revelation or religious experience tells us anything about reality? It would be unphilosophical to rule such an enquiry out at the start.

5.23 But, says the critic, that is just why philosophy is such a snare. It makes us ask questions about revelation which ought never to be asked. But again it must be repeated (1.3) that the educated person cannot allow himself to be schizophrenic. It is surely necessary for the religious person to whom such questions occur and of whom such questions are asked to be able to supply something like an intelligent answer.

5.24 Nevertheless, the critic has some justice on his side. It amounts to this. A radical questioning of the validity of religious experience should not overlook the fact that religion constitutes a dynamic and central part of the history of men. Therefore, good reasons ought to be given for being sceptical of the tradition that men can gain some insight in experience into the nature of the transcendent. It is not just blind conservatism which holds that it would be strange indeed if all such visions and experiences were entirely delusory. It is therefore reasonable to approach the matter in a rather cautious way. It would be wrong to follow the example of, say, Freud, and base the view that religion is illusory on speculative ideas in psychology and a grossly distorted account of prehistory. Are the walls of Jericho to tumble at such a weak and home-made trumpet?

5.25 A further important point of method is this. If we are mainly looking at revelation as religious experience, we are necessarily concerned centrally with the deliverances of the more important figures of religious history, with the Jeremiahs, the Pauls, the Buddhas. We are not basing important truths of religion on my feeble intuitions or my neighbour's faltering visions. These may be personally important. But we are not either so presumptuous or democratic as to suppose that God must reveal himself in an intense and illuminating way in each individual heart. Necessarily, then, ours is a rather 'aristocratic' approach. This is the only realistic way of tackling the problem, by looking to the focal points in religious histories. We are more in the position of critics than of artists, ordinary people who may recognize revelation, but are not the immediate recipients of it. I am not, of course, in the comparison with artists suggesting that people like Jeremiah themselves, as religious geniuses, *created* the revelation: for was it not a feature of such explosively numinous experiences that they seemed to come spontaneously and, as it were, from 'outside'?

5.26 But the word 'outside' raises some acute philosophical problems. We may believe that a perception is in part caused by the object perceived, and that an experience which does not have such an outside source is illusory. For instance, the alcoholic who sees pink rats is suffering from an hallucination precisely because outside there in the room there are no pink rats. What causes his hallucination comes from 'inside' him (whisky may be the cause, but only on condition that it first gets inside him!). Likewise, it may be argued that if a perception of the divine Being is to be genuine, it must be in part caused by something lying outside the individual, namely by God. But here the real trouble starts. For the daffodil I perceive is literally outside me: it is at a different point in space from me. But God is not in space, and so cannot be literally outside me. There is another trouble, too: for the rather naïve view that the cause of a true perception lies outside me raises difficulties about me. If I include my body, then it is false that true perceptions must have part-causes outside me. I can truly perceive, through certain organs of feeling, that there is a lot of food in my stomach. But my stomach is inside me. But if we mean by me the mind, then there is a difficulty in speaking of things being literally inside or outside my mind, since the mind is not a spatial object in the ordinary sense.

5.27 Consequently, we must refine our ideas about the causes of perception. Perhaps as follows: by saying that for a perception to be genuine, the object of my perception, that is, the thing which I believe myself to be perceiving, must be part-cause of my experience. Thus, for instance, if we introduced some pink rats into the alcoholic's room, but if, too, he would have seen pink rats anyway, we would be somewhat reluctant to say that he really saw the real pink rats. By analogy, we may want to say that if an experience is a genuine experience of God, God must be part-cause at least of that experience.

5.28   But this in turn raises other problems. For if God is creator of the whole cosmos, then he is certainly part-cause of any supposed experience of him. The condition is automatically fulfilled. But this does not seem satisfactory as an answer to our problem. For if, it may well be held, an experience of God is entirely caused by prior causes in the world – mundane causes – then it is suspect. If a vision has psychological causes (we may think) then it can be written off. Rather, we want assurances that at least some religious experiences are in some sense directly caused by God.

5.29   The phrase 'at least some' is important. For it may be objected to the whole line of approach in this discussion that you can have genuine knowledge without its being directly caused by its object. For instance, a piece of mathematical knowledge is not mysteriously caused by numbers existing outside the individual. Similarly, if a person at a service finds, in the ceremony and the fellowship, a heightened awareness of God's grace, isn't this something genuine, even if we do not think that there is some kind of direct intervention by God? Or if a theologian reaches a correct conclusion about a matter of doctrine, is this not genuine knowledge? Yet, nevertheless, surely it is supposed in the great religions that the 'aristocratic' experiences (5.25) are somehow specially caused by God. Moreover, we must distinguish between knowledge *that* and knowledge *of*. I can know that such and such is the case: but this is not some kind of perceptual experience. But knowledge of a person, encountering him, does directly involve perceptual experience. The theologian knows *that* such-and-such is the case; but this does not imply that the theologian must necessarily have had any direct knowledge *of* God. And in talking of religious experience it is knowledge *of* that we are chiefly concerned with.

5.30   Perhaps part of the solution of our problem will come to us if we consider religious experience in the first instance simply from the human side. Bearing in mind our earlier conclusions about creativity, could we think of the great religious deliverances, for instance those of the Old Testament prophets, as examples of creative novelty? Certainly the same sort of conditions are present as in the case of scientific and artistic discovery. For there is a certain range of experience and activity (religion) and within this pattern of conscious response to the numinous there breaks in something which goes beyond what was before. The vivid and powerful awareness of something supremely holy which the prophets displayed goes beyond earlier ideas and responses. Similarly, that religion itself which the prophets did so much to shape was later transcended in the work and teaching of Christ. In both cases, there was in existence already a body of tradition which was necessary to the later developments which in part rendered the body of tradition obsolete. Here, then, in the sphere of religious experience there is something like the creative novelty which we can find elsewhere in human progress.

5.31 So far we are looking at the matter simply from the human side. But already we have some intimation that it may be quite wrong to think that a causal account of the great experiences of religion can be given. But still (it will be objected), how are we to know whether these creative developments are not *merely* human? It may be that, as well as having a genius in the arts, men also have a genius for the numinous. Every so often sudden uprushes of religious feeling take on a creative form and supersede what went before. But so what?

5.32 The critic might indeed go further. If men can have a creative genius for fiction, why not also have a genius for making myths about a transcendent world? It may be that religion is a superbly elaborate kind of self-deception. And if men can be creative in good, remember, too, that they can be creative in evil: and both the discovery of truth and the creation of falsehood are human gifts.

5.33 But we can reply: to what end does the deception take place? It is true that priests have often manipulated sacred knowledge for their own benefit, and that it often looks as though certain doctrines play a role in keeping society together in a certain form. And there is no doubt that some myths are the product of deep psychological urges. But even when all this is taken into account, it still remains a fact that religion does involve its own kind of experiences and inner logic, and these still have to be accounted for. If the numinous experience, for example, is distinct from other forms of human consciousness, then how can it simply be derived from them, on the assumption that numinous creativity is a kind of self-deception? For if it arises to deal with psychological or social problems, no doubt in an unconscious way, then why does it have its own peculiar character?

5.34 Of course, if one has already made up one's mind that the universe has no transcendent source and no transcendent side to it, that the only reality is the observable cosmos, then no doubt it will be easier to think that religion arises out of psychological and other urges, even though the special character of numinous experience so far remains unaccounted for. It is something of a gamble either way: it is a leap to believe in the transcendent, and it is a leap to believe that somehow in theory religious experience could be given some kind of natural explanation. But all this underlines once again the importance of natural theology (1.12), for in giving us some hint that the cosmos is created, even if such a hint is in no sense a proof, if it does provide some rational ground for refusing to see the cosmos as the whole of reality.

5.35 But then, once the leap is made, towards some kind of belief in the transcendent, the importance of religious experience is bound to strike us powerfully. For it is not as though the prophets' experiences can be merely regarded as a form of human creativity, since it is implicit in their visions, their awareness of the holy, that they should ascribe them to an 'outside' source. Moreover, this 'outside' source is outside in a strange way, for it (or he) lies somehow beyond or behind the objects in the environment of the prophet. The holy Being is 'present' as though in the environment of the prophet, and yet somehow also it is concealed by the environment. This suggestion that the holy Being is 'beyond' what is seen in space and time fits in with the metaphysical idea of a creator 'outside' the cosmos.

But it would be wrong to think that our thinking need operate only in this direction – beginning with the metaphysical idea and then, on that basis, seeing the validity of religious experience: equally we might move the other way, and judge metaphysics by the yardstick of religious experience. Suffice it to say that the two approaches fit together, and that they lend each other mutual support.

5.36 It is crucial, then, if we are to believe in the possibility of genuine religious experience, to accept in principle the idea of a transcendent being or state. But even so isn't it theoretically possible that though such a being exists it is not the cause of the actual religious experiences of the great religious figures of history? May it not be that, exalted as their encounters were, they were after all encounters with nothing at all? The idea is just possible: and yet it is a curious position to take up, as though one were saying 'Yes, there can be an encounter with the transcendent Being, and yet we can disregard the testimony of the great figures of religious history.' For what reason can they be disregarded? Of course, someone who had himself had some superior experience and insight into God's nature might wish to say that all other teachers were deluded: but in that case, at least one such encounter is regarded as valid and genuine.

5.37 Further, the possibility that religious experience can tell us something about the transcendent world reinforces the adapted form of the Teleological Argument which we used earlier (4.55). For suppose that the capacity for creative novelty has arisen among conscious beings in an otherwise blind cosmos; suppose, further, that the most dynamic novelty, one which has permeated and transformed moral and other values, is the recognition of the transcendent world beyond this one; then we can add religion to the values which the development of human consciousness allows to come into existence.

5.38 So far, then, we have considered the general reasons which might be given for holding that religious experience can point towards the truth. Nevertheless, it is a perplexing fact that different religious 'geniuses' and teachers have said different things on the

basis of their encounters with the transcendent world. By consequence, the great religions of the world teach doctrines which are
apparently incompatible with one another. This fact strikes us very
forcibly today, because of increased knowledge of the great Eastern
religions, and of the shrinking of the world due to modern communi-
cations. Thus the ordinary man may well complain that if religion
brings us truth, it does so in an intolerably obscure and confused
way. Why should not everyone be given direct and clear evidence
of the existence of the transcendent? Then there would be no need
for all these worries.

5.39   The answer can perhaps be given in the form of a kind of
quantitative parable which is reminiscent of what we discovered
earlier (2.53). God cannot show himself all the time and too much,
for then he becomes indistinguishable from the regularities of the
natural cosmos. He cannot, on the other hand, fail to show himself
at all, or men have no knowledge of him. Not much, but not never.
The human sense of the numinous, by shuddering at the uncanny
and mysterious, prepares mankind for recognizing divinity in what
is unusual. And that is where God has to show himself. But this,
of course, is only a kind of parable.

5.40   Another is this. The full self-disclosure of God must be an
overwhelming event. For God to overwhelm us continually would
deprive us of our freedom and capacity to love him. No man, it is
said, shall see God and live. This is an exaggeration of the same
point.

5.41   Furthermore, the unusual and rare nature of the higher experiences of religion is something which religions have traditionally
recorded. It is not for everyone to be a Buddha or Eckhart. But
religions have not claimed that such revelations are rare in order
to get round modern philosophical difficulties or to cheat the em-
piricists. And if we want to know about the nature of religion, we
have to listen to the deliverances of religion. For the manifestations
of God to be common-or-garden occurrences religious thought
through the ages would have to be radically other than it has been.
In a way, asking why it should not be other is like asking: 'Why do

we use the concept *good* when talking about morality?' Anyone who understands what morals is sees this concept as being central. Anyone who understands what religion is sees that it is in the nature of the case for God to manifest himself mysteriously.

5.42 But, says the critic, if this is so, ought we not to be agnostics? The reasonable man proportions his belief to the evidence. If the evidence is highly ambiguous (as you are claiming), then he should say neither 'Yea' nor 'Nay'.

5.43 The answer to this is twofold. First, though there must be ambiguity in the evidences of revealed religion, this does not mean that it is unreasonable to accept them. For general considerations, such as we have here been outlining, may incline us to accept the authority of the great figures in religion. And second, every view of the world, every *Weltanschauung*, has the property of being somewhat doubtful. There are no absolutely knock-down arguments in favour of Marxism or of physiological materialism (3.25) or of Buddhism. That is to say, you can find dispassionate and intelligent men who would have some reasons for denying any of these positions. But this does not entail that these positions are all false. Nor does it entail that it is rational to suspend judgment completely. For when it comes to a *Weltanschauung*, there is no way of escape. The way we think, talk and behave is partly determined by prior assumptions about the nature of reality. And it is important to know where one stands. It is therefore necessary to adopt a view about reality, even though it is a hard business. Of course if all views were absolutely equally plausible and there could be no rational way of choosing between them, then you could toss a coin. But it wouldn't matter which way it fell, for if there were really nothing to choose between the views they would all amount to the same thing! So there must remain the necessity of answering some such questions as 'What think ye of Christ?'

5.44 But though we can give this kind of general defence of the validity of the experience of the transcendent, there still remains the question as to how we are to determine which of the great religions represents the highest truth. We have already seen (5.10) the extent to which they vary in their central beliefs and how these latter are considerably determined by the emphasis placed on the two great types of religious experience. But amid these conflicting revelations how are we to see our way to the truth?

5.45   A Christian might think that the answer to this was fairly straightforward. After all, he might say, we know that the Christian religion is true because of certain historical events. It is a faith firmly based on history and that settles the matter. Yet, as we have seen (2.50), Christianity cannot be proved metahistorically. Some reasons for this have been given but it is useful to dwell further on this point. First, as we pointed out earlier, underlying belief in Christ there is belief in a personal God, the God of the Jews. We cannot understand 'I and the Father are one' unless we understand who the Father is. Thus a presupposition of interpreting the events of the New Testament in a Christian sense is belief in theism. Second, the Bible incorporates a view about the importance of history which is not shared among all religions and which may require separate defence. Third, the central acts of Christ's life are not simply historical. If Christ conquered death in virtue of his resurrection, then he has performed something that goes beyond the limits of merely historical enquiry. For the conquest of death, in this sense, is a cosmic, not just an historical event. The notion of his redeeming men through his sacrifice upon the Cross is another case in point. Thus the spiritual significance of various acts of Christ's life is not something that can be simply derived from an investigation of historical evidence. The acts presuppose certain central ideas, like sacrifice, which need to be shown to be valid ones. Fourth, as we saw (2.49), claim that Christianity can be proved just by doing some historical research would break down because of modern developments. We are now inclined to be a bit more sceptical of historical reports and especially when they deal with such controversial events as those described in the New Testament. So there is room for doubting the correctness of the Gospel narratives; and it is no longer sufficient, as a way of proving something, to turn up a Bible and point to the appropriate chapter and verse. But for our present purpose, it is the first three of these points which will loom largest.

5.46 How, then, amid the great faiths do we tell where the fullest statement of the truth lies? The choice initially lies between three great systems of belief. First, there is theism, the belief in a personal Creator who reveals himself to men: represented by Judaism, Islam and Christianity, as well as by certain tendencies in Hindu thought, such as the theology of the *Bhagavadgita*. Then second, at the other extreme, there is the agnostic faith of Theravada Buddhism. And third, in the great Hindu teacher Shankara, there is an intermediate kind of doctrine and one which is not too unlike some of the main teachings of Mahayana Buddhism. Shankara's theology underlies much contemporary Hindu apologetic, and is not without its influence among some Western intellectuals who are dissatisfied with the rather (as they think) arrogant and exclusive claims of Christianity.

5.47 Briefly, Shankara's doctrines are as follows. The key to the Upanishads is the famous phrase 'That art thou', which sums up the idea, mentioned above (5.9), that the eternal element within man, the Atman, is in highest truth identical with the sacred Power, Brahman, which pervades and sustains the cosmos. Taking the phrase to its logical conclusion Shankara argues that there is only one Reality, and that any idea that the soul is distinct from this divine Absolute, or that the world is real independently of it, rests upon an illusion. Nevertheless, from the standpoint of the ordinary man who has not attained to full enlightenment, it is possible to speak as though the Absolute is the creator of the world, and to worship God as a personal being. Thus Shankara makes use of the idea of two levels of truth. In highest truth there is only one Reality, and all the rest is illusion. But at a lower level, that Reality manifests itself as a personal Lord and Creator, distinct from the cosmos and from me. Shankara's idea of different levels is extensively used by modern Hindus, who treat the various religions of the world as being true at a lower level: they must ultimately be transcended in the mystical knowledge that there is but one divine Reality. In this way, Hinduism, which includes so many kinds of religious practices and ideals, can claim to be able to fulfil the great religions of the world and to harmonize them. But needless to say, the essential Hindu doctrines represented by Shankara are not themselves compatible with the claims of personal theism, nor for that matter can they be accepted by the Theravada Buddhist, who would be disinclined to think of nirvana as a kind of divine Absolute. It is interesting to note that there are some strong resemblances between Shankara's teachings and those of Meister Eckhart, the most controversial of Christian mystics. It is also interesting to remember that one of Otto's best works, *Mysticism East and West*, is concerned with a comparison between the two teachers.

5.48 But what are we to say about these three great forms of faith? How could anyone decide which is true? Or, at least, which approximates most closely to the truth? First, as to theism: what are the grounds, from the standpoint of religious experience, for thinking it to be true? It gives, of course, the highest and most intense expression to the sense of the numinous, and thereby, too, can hope to incorporate the insights of morality. But when we are faced with Buddhism or the teachings of Shankara and of the Upanishads, what are we to say? I think we could criticize both the rigid monotheism of early Islam and the purely contemplative form of Buddhism on the ground that neither does justice to the other variety of religious experience. Theravada Buddhism has no place for a Jeremiah: early Islam has no place for a Buddha. Thus a comprehensive faith will be one which mingles together the two great strands of experience and language. And since we must respect the deliverances of the great mystics, both East and West; and since too it would be, given that we accept any authority at all, absurd to neglect the deeds and sayings of the great prophets, it follows that, if anything gives the truth, it must be a form of faith which harmoniously combines the two types of spirituality. And indeed it is an interesting comment on the history of the great religions that Buddhism itself went on to develop a numinous aspect, in some of the forms of Mahayana Buddhism; while Islam went on to develop a mystical side, in Sufism. Buddhism grew into a kind of theism; while Islam developed a type of mysticism. But then what are we to say about the great Hindu doctrine that the Self and God are one? Why not agree that the highest reality is the Absolute, one's identity with which one can realize in inner experience? Surely Shankara and the Upanishads can claim a mingling of the contemplative and the numinous. And so they have as good a claim to the truth as does theism. The only difference is that the doctrine of a spiritual Absolute, by relegating the notion of God as personal creator and dispenser of grace to the realm of a lower and incomplete truth, definitely stresses more the importance of the mystical than of the numinous. A further sign of this is the abolition of that 'dualism' (5.4) between worshipper and object of worship, between ultimate Reality and man, which typifies the idea of the numinous. And because of this emphasis on the contemplative aspect of religion, the idea of a personal God is thought to be ultimately illusory.

5.49 It is therefore no exaggeration to claim that such an emphasis ends by destroying the numinous side of religion. Nor is it surprising that Shankara the theologian who so subtly and profoundly elaborated the theology of non-dualism, as it is called, was accused in his time of being a crypto-Buddhist. For any real value in theism fades away, in his system of thought, and one approximates to the austerer doctrines of early Buddhism. In brief, if the mystical and numinous elements in religion are to be combined in a single system of doctrine, the mystical side cannot be emphasized too much without swallowing up and destroying the other. If we take the contemplative's claim to achieve identity with the transcendent too literally, we sacrifice the insights of the prophet. It seems therefore that the proper way to combine the two strands of experience so that the value of each is preserved is to express them through the theology of theism. This is done, for instance, in that great Indian religious classic the *Bhagavadgita*; and is done supremely well in Christian theology, which finds a place for the mystical path. The great Christian mystics retain the sense of closeness to God without claiming literal identity, and can express their experience in such terms as those of spiritual marriage. As man and wife, though remaining two persons, become 'one flesh' and cleave together, so the soul and God come together in intimate union, yet remain separate entities. Thus we can conclude, from this necessarily brief and crude survey, that theism is the doctrine best fitted to combine the two strands of religious language and practice. This conclusion is quite apart from any considerations drawn from natural theology in the ordinary sense. It is quite apart from the reasonings that hitherto we have been conducting here, about the Cosmological and Teleological Arguments.

5.50   As to the value and importance of history (5.45), this is in some degree linked to belief in theism. For the idea of a personal Creator carries with it the idea of his creating through an act of will analogous to a human decision. This in turn expresses well the sense of radical contingency that afflicts one when contemplating the possibility that nothing might have existed (4.16). Now an act of will is figured mythologically as like an historical act. God's momentous creative act is pictured as being like some tremendous historical decision, like Caesar's crossing the Rubicon. Thus already in the idea of a personal Creator there are elements which link God and history. On the other hand, in mystical religion there is a tendency to turn away from the ordinary concerns of the world, so much so that the world may come to be regarded as impermanent and even illusory, as somehow without any real substance. It is perhaps, therefore, natural that Indian religion, with its strongly contemplative emphasis, should often look upon history as cyclical. Mythologically this is sometimes pictured as though everything to the tiniest detail has happened countless times before. But for the theist, believing in a dualism between God and the world and between God and the soul, the cosmos and conscious beings are independent (or relatively independent) entities, existing as it were in their own right apart from God. So the theist has to believe in the reality of the cosmos and of persons. And human persons are creative. They bring to birth new values, new forms of existence. But a cyclical view of history tends to destroy this notion. For there would then be nothing new under the sun. It will be seen, then, that a valuation of history, though not strictly to be deduced from theistic belief, is a natural corollary of it. It fits.

5.51   It should be noted that the present argument for theism, depending on the principle that a true faith must be comprehensive and must incorporate the important data of religious experience, both numinous and mystical, and depending too on insights drawn from the history of religion, is not simply a matter of measuring other faiths by the yardstick of one's own faith and finding them wanting. It is easy enough to 'prove' that other faiths are false if you begin with certain assumptions derived from one's own faith. Judged by the revelation believed in by one tradition, other revelations are false or defective. Rather, we have been trying to give more 'neutral' reasons for faith in theism. But again it should be stressed that these points which have been made in no sense constitute knock-down arguments: and we must not forget the points to be made the other way; for instance, the wonderful simplicity of Theravada doctrine, in its central affirmations, may well be attractive to those who in any case find intellectual and other difficulties in believing in a personal God. The problem of evil, which we shall discuss in the next chapter, should not be forgotten, and it is a powerful counter-argument against theism. But even so, judging just from the data of religious experience, there is, as we have seen, a great deal to be said for the type of theism that can give a place to the mystical quest.

5.52 But theism, as well as having a place for the intimate union between saints and God in the mystical quest, has an inner dynamism which also leads, but in a different way, to a closer harmony between God and man. We have already noted (5.5) that as part of its 'inner logic' the numinous experience issues in a sense of the sinfulness and unholiness of the worshipper, by contrast with the holy Being with whom he is confronted. The sense of sin is reinforced by the undoubted moral and other failings of human beings: though their life, initially constricted by the demands of the painful evolutionary struggle towards greater freedom and knowledge, was bound to involve imperfection, nevertheless in gaining freedom men are also well aware that that freedom has in part been abused. The ignorance and suffering have been greater than they need have been, and the creation of god in human society has been echoed by the refinements of evil which humans have discovered. So, not merely at the level of the pure numinous feeling, of the awe which a person feels when confronted by the overpowering majesty of the transcendent Holy One, but also at the level of morality, men feel their puniness and guilt.

5.53 The feeling of moral inadequacy is no doubt reinforced for the believer in a personal God by the fact, as we have seen (5.50), that in theism the world counts. It is no illusion, as Shankara maintains. Its importance is seen in the very fact that God and the world are (for the theist) distinct. The cosmos, in existing independently, testifies to the independent importance attached to it by the Creator. Thus again theism is well adapted, so to speak, to the incorporation within itself of the highest moral values.

5.54 But the sense of sin and inadequacy, which flows from men's confrontation with the purity and majesty of God, itself creates a problem. Salvation must come from God, for only the one holy being can confer holiness upon others. And yet, on the other hand, men feel the need to do something about their condition. They wish to expiate their sin. So, too, if I have wronged a friend and wish to make it up, I feel called upon to make a concrete gesture of some sort to show my contrition and renewed desire for his love. But in the context of theism this represents a paradox; only men can expiate, and only God can save.

5.55 This paradox is resolved in a strangely wonderful way by Christianity. For Christ, in being both God and man, is alone in a position to fulfil this paradox. His self-sacrifice expiates on behalf of men, and because he is truly human. His power to save springs from his being truly God. Though the Incarnation is at first sight a blasphemous doctrine – for is it not blasphemous to think that a man could be God? – and though it adds a severe complication to theology – for is not the Trinity doctrine most difficult to expound? – nevertheless it fits in with the whole pattern of theistic beliefs. And it fits, too, into history.

5.56 But yet it must be objected, and from the standpoint of Christian belief, that this is altogether a peculiar defence of Christianity: for Christ here seems to be something of an afterthought tagged on to theistic belief. But still there is something quite right in order of exposition. For the whole of Christ's work in reconciling God and man can make no sense unless belief in a personal God is already accepted. In discussing the choice between the formulations of the various great religions it is obviously necessary first to validate the idea of theism.

5.57 But still the objection retains some force. For although the idea of Christ's self-sacrifice is in part at least derived from older ways of looking at men's relationship to the supreme God, it also transforms theism itself. God as creator and object of worship must be seen in the light of Christ, just as Christ must be seen in the light of pure theism. Likewise, Christ's life and teachings transform our views of morality. Thus, Christ's life and death must themselves be seen as a new creative act, in which new forces are released into history.

5.58 But it is at this point that a new type of evidence is relevant. Hitherto we have been discussing religious truth from the standpoint of religious experience. But the metahistorical (2.48) claims made by Christianity are of a different quality. Though the bare historical facts are not sufficient to demonstrate Christ's divinity, they are necessary elements in that belief. But here we leave the field of religious experience, though as we have seen the 'logic' of religious experience is highly relevant to beliefs about the Incarnation. We note that with the introduction of historical criteria to judge (in part) the claims of Christianity, a new dimension is added to the contents of religious truth.

5.59 Some difficulty, however, may be felt about the picture of revelation which emerges from this account. For it is implicit in the way in which we have approached religious experience and the revelations of other faiths that the great religions all contain quite a strong element of truth, even if Judaeo-Christian theism represents the highest expression of divine truth. But does not this imply that God revealed himself too in the experience of the Buddha? But if so, why not more clearly? Why was the Buddha left to preach contemplation and the insights of mysticism, while at the same time being agnostic about a personal Creator? For that matter, why *should* there be two ways to the highest experience of God? Why should there be a division between the prophetic and mystical experiences? Earlier (5.8 ff.) we gave reasons for saying that there are two forms of religious experience, and briefly indicated the evidence that the two forms in fact exist; but yet it may be asked, 'Why should it be so? Does God put himself in two different disguises? Does he adapt himself to the monk and to the prophet?'

5.60   There does not appear to be any easy answer to these questions, though certain points are relevant. First, if God is to appear in an historical setting there is an inevitable scandal of particularity, and this would imply that the 'build-up' for the full revelation of God would involve specially striking self-disclosures of God to the prophets, and so on. Second, the existence of various religions may, up to a point, be part of the divine plan, since without variation in religion men could not learn to appreciate the full force of the true faith. A 'closed' religious system, which does not have to pay attention to rival claims of truth, tends to lose its insights. Heresies themselves have played an important part in the apprehension of Christian truth. Indeed the present confrontation between the great religions may well prove as significant an epoch in Christian history as was the fruitful meeting between the Church and Ancient Greece. Third, a distinction has to be made between experience and interpretation (5.9). Though the great experiences may suggest certain ways of describing them, it is scarcely to be thought that God treats men as puppets and, as it were, feeds in the correct interpretation plus the doctrinal superstructure so that the recipient of a higher insight can make no mistakes. By consequence, and fourthly, it would be wrong to adopt an over-literal picture of God deciding to show this bit of himself to Jeremiah, that bit to St Paul and another bit to the Buddha.

5.61   Our argument, then, has been designed to show that there can be reasons for holding that one religion is true (or, if you like, truer than the others). Necessarily the outline of these reasons has been all too brief: and much more can be said. In this sense, some answer has been given to the question: 'What reasons are there for choosing one religion rather than another?' But, of course, as we have also seen (5.18), it would be quite unrealistic to think that normally the individual is faced with such a choice, as a real live option. For undoubtedly for most people the formative influence of their own culture and tradition makes it improbable that they should seriously contemplate changing to another culture and tradition. Yet now, when the world's cultures are beginning to mingle together, the issues raised here will be increasingly important. Let us hope that there will be a genuine dialogue of religions at the highest level.

5.62 We can now draw together the threads of our whole argument up to now, and see what kind of picture of the world it presents. Both in regard to miracles, and in regard to free will, we argued against a rigidly 'closed' view of reality, as though everything needs to be governed by causal regularities. At least the theoretical possibility of God's miraculous intervention in the world must be allowed: and a proper explanation of free will may mean that we use some such idea as that of creativity. This in turn renews hope in the possibility of arguing for God's existence. For if there is to be an explanation of the existence of the cosmos, it must be non-scientific, and yet at the same time intelligible. The idea of human creativity fulfils both these requirements, so that we can think of the Cause of the cosmos by analogy with the way in which humanity sometimes transcends the regularities in which it is embedded. Once we make this leap of explanation, we can also make use of the facts to which the Teleological Argument draws attention, for the comparative orderliness of the cosmos does indeed look significant when we see that it is sufficient to allow the evolution of conscious and rational beings, who thereby confer value upon what otherwise would be dead and meaningless. Nevertheless, such solutions to the problems thrown up by the existence and orderliness of the cosmos remain rather thin unless they are joined to belief in revelation. The mistake of some philosophers, and notably Kant, is to ignore this possibility of an encounter with the transcendent. Religious experience has to be examined. We then went on to give reasons for thinking that this may provide a valid avenue of knowledge about reality, and to see how theism can be defended in the context of the world's religions.

5.63 Our total picture has been an evolutionary one: of the world as being created as a theatre for the production of human and other values, an arena for the exercise of creativity. But the possibility of a genuine encounter between men and God through God's self-revelation gives this evolutionary picture a deeper significance. For it is as if men's knowledge of God is itself evolutionary. From dim beginnings, men have struggled upward towards this higher knowledge; and the struggle is not finished yet. True, the Christian may say that God's self-revelation in Christ is in some sense final. But the significance of this event is not exhausted by the traditional formulations of the Church. Already, just because our world-picture has changed, partly through the progress of science, men cannot help seeing God and Christ in a new light. This means that the philosophy of religion itself has an important part to play in clarifying and revaluing theology, for the philosopher, as we have seen, operates a lot of the time on the borders between different areas of human knowledge and inquiry. And neither religion nor theology can afford to ignore what goes on beyond those various frontiers. This is already obvious from the fact that Evolutionary Theory has had such a considerable impact upon religious thinking.

5.64 Our treatment of religious experience, springing from the work of Rudolf Otto, allowed us to consider the issue of the truth of the various religions. But we have already noted that the problem of evil is a great stumbling-block to belief in theism, even if on the grounds of natural theology and of religious experience and history that belief may seem reasonable. The evolutionary picture perhaps makes the position more acute. For God, in making a cosmos where conscious beings have to grope their way forward, is almost bound to inflict suffering upon animals and men. What can the theologian or philosopher say in face of this terrible fact?

6

F. R. Tennant and the Problem of Evil

6.1 I f God is both good and omnipotent, how can it be that there is evil in the cosmos which he has created? The Buddha, whose refusal to affirm or to deny belief in God may seem strange and para-doxical to Westerners, was deeply impressed by the fact of suffering; and this indeed was probably one of his reasons for ignoring the idea of a Creator. This is one instance among many of the fact that the problem of evil is not something which people just use as a debating point against Christians: it is often the great stumbling-block preventing belief in God among people of deep moral sensitivity. It is therefore not to be shrugged off lightly. For this reason it is most important to try to tackle it in a clear and sober manner. For obscurity and pious hopes may well be interpreted as signs that one is avoiding the real issue. In the following pages, I shall partly be following some suggestions made by F. R. Tennant in his *Philo-sophical Theology* in sketching out a way of dealing with the prob-lem. Here above all was a theologian and philosopher who preferred sobriety and rationality in the attempt to establish the truth of theism, and his regard for science meant that he tried squarely to face problems in Christian belief which have arisen since Evolu-tionary Theory has called in doubt the literal story of Adam.

6.2 It happens too that the problem of evil has figured quite pro-minently in recent discussions of religious truth and language; and it will be necessary to make some allusion to these matters. For in-

stance, it has been argued that because Christians, while affirming
that God is love, refuse to consider the facts of evil and suffering as
evidence against that claim, they are evacuating their affirmation of
any real meaning. For a statement which could not be shown, in any
circumstances, to be false, by reference to the observed facts, is, so
it has been held, meaningless. Thus in this chapter we shall not
merely be engaged in the more traditional problems associated with
the problem which Tennant thirty years ago was concerned to
tackle; but also we shall be attacking the newer philosophical
issues which have arisen since his time.

6.3 The problem of evil is, of course, only a real problem for one
who believes in God. Or more particularly, it is a problem for one
who believes that God is good, omnipotent and omniscient. (But
perhaps it is more convenient to include God's omniscience more
simply under his omnipotence; for a God who can do anything, but
does not always know what is the best way of doing it, might be
said to be, in an important sense, less than all-powerful.) For clearly,
if God can do anything, and yet in fact produces a cosmos in which
there is suffering and evil, then there must be something wrong with
his intentions. Conversely, if he be good, and there is nothing
wrong with his intentions, and yet he produces a world where in
fact there is evil and suffering, then there must be some deficiency
in his power. Both conclusions would be repugnant to Christian
doctrine. For not only do Christians believe that God is supremely
good and that he is indeed the source of values (4.55): but also
the doctrine that God created the world out of nothing most
emphatically emphasizes God's omnipotence. It is not as though,
like the gods conceived in some other systems of theology, such as
Plato's, God was limited by the brute properties of matter, and
could therefore merely impose form on it without being able to rid
it of its chaotic tendencies. No, God has created the cosmos out of
nothing: he created the matter as well as the form in which it has
been moulded.

6.4 Nor can we evade the issue by saying that perhaps after all
evil does not really exist, that it is an illusion. It might be claimed
that from the standpoint of eternity, what we think of as evil really

is not so at all. But this does not prevent us from finding actual pain and cruelty in the world; it is these that are our data, and it is a mere subterfuge to postulate some eternal standpoint from which we can wish them away. If I am foolish to imagine that I am suffering, that scarcely helps me. For imagining that one is suffering is bad enough, and to be told that I am mistaken in so imagining it makes it worse.

6.5 Equally futile is the attempt to say that evil is something merely negative. Just as blindness is the absence of sight, so (it has been argued) evils in general are not positive existences; but we use the word 'evil' to refer to gaps in what should be, deficiencies of good, rather than presences of bad. This is to ignore the fact that when I feel toothache or when a rat squirms in pain we are quite right to speak of actual feelings and states of affairs. These are as much there to be experienced as thrills of pleasure and jumps of joy.

6.6 Nor will it do just to try and diminish the amount of suffering and evil. Some are inclined to say: 'But look, pain is useful; it tells you when your tooth is decaying; it teaches you not to play with fire.' True, and this is an important point in its way. But not all pain is useful: not all produces a greater good. So the move only results in something like this: whereas we thought previously that there were x units of suffering in the cosmos, we now find that there are only $\frac{2}{3}x$. God, in short, is evil, but not as evil as we thought. This is but cold comfort for the Christian.

6.7 It will have been noticed that mostly I have been talking about suffering; and most of suffering in the cosmos is naturally produced. That is, it is not due to human wickedness. Nevertheless, of course, there is still quite a lot of evil caused in the latter way. Since, however, the two sorts of suffering raise rather different problems it is convenient to make a distinction between them and to label them differently. The first kind of evil (suffering arising from natural causes) is often called 'physical evil', since it is produced by the constitution of the physical world. The second sort (evil due to human wickedness) is often called 'moral evil'. The problems about the origins of each can to some extent be dealt with separately; and it is probably more illuminating to deal with the second first.

6.8 It may, however, be noted that speculative theologians can try to assimilate the two cases, by saying that the physical evils in the cosmos (or at least those which seem to be superfluous and unproductive of good) are the consequence of some cosmic fall. The whole universe has somehow gone awry due to the fall of Satan. Thus physical evil is due to wickedness, and so is a species of moral evil. Indeed, there are passages in the New Testament which support this view. Still, it does not seem to be a good way out of the difficulty. For first, it is too speculative, in pushing the origin of evil to some event in a transcendent realm. And second, it is exceedingly hard to understand how God should have allowed his wonderful creation to be infected in this manner. Is the whole creation to be ruined just to give freedom to the angels?

6.9 But it could be answered that after all this idea of a cosmic fall is only a logical extension of belief in Satan. If the Devil tempts men, was indeed instrumental in the fall of Adam, maliciously combats the saving work of God, if he does these things then already God is allowing a very considerable interference with his creation. But even so there seems something intolerable in the belief that millions upon millions of living beings should be sacrificed to the evil power of Satan. And to what end? In any event, belief in the Devil is steadily fading among Christians, except as a symbolic way of representing the many obstacles to goodness, freedom and devotion to God. It is doubtful whether something cast into such an archaic story-form will succeed in dispelling the genuine perplexities with which the existence of moral and physical evil confronts us.

6.10 So then, if we are not going to invoke a cosmic fall which has infected the creation, the problems of moral and physical evil remain separate. As we said, we shall start with moral evil. At first, this appears to be the less intractable problem. For moral evil is the consequence of the acts of responsible beings (by definition, indeed). But responsible beings are free, and God, in bestowing this freedom, would be grossly inconsistent if he were for ever interfering with it to prevent particular evils. And what would the freedom only to do good amount to? Thus, there seems to be a ready-made answer to the problem. Moral evil has come into the world because God has created free beings. The evil should be imputed to the latter, and not to God. Of course, it might still be felt that this does not explain all. Why should God submit the other animals to the peril of being confronted by men – men who could and do exercise their freedom to kill, and sometimes to torture, their fellow-animals? So more must be said: it must be said that, for all that, the risk was worth taking, that the responsible, moral, creative being would constitute the crown of creation. We shall return to this point shortly.

6.11 However – and here we come to a recent argument against theism – if determinism and free will are compatible (a position which we discussed earlier (3.14)) there would seem to be no inconsistency in God's having created men both perfectly good *and* free. Against this, we may deploy such arguments as we have already given for saying that the above position is false. But it is worth pointing out, too, that, even if we adopted it, it is not at all clear that any alternative world, so far as we can imagine it, would be better than this present one. For the determinist must believe that the tendency of men to fall for certain sorts of temptations is due to the way in which men are constructed. To make men immune to these temptations, they would have to be radically reconstructed. A little fiction may illustrate the point. Suppose that the alternative cosmos we are envisaging operated according to roughly the same laws as does the present one. How would men, in such a world, have to be built if they were never to steal, never to commit adultery and the like? Would they have to be such that a man became inevitably infatuated with the first uninfatuated girl he met, and conversely? And that people arrived in the world each with his own store of provisions, of such a nature that another person's things seemed repellent to oneself? It does not take much of such fictionalizing to see that we would end up with very peculiar creatures. Would they be truly human? Still, they might be better than us, so let us not worry about that. Yes, but would they be good? If there is a temptation which I have no chance of falling for, such is my con-

stitution, then how can it really be called a temptation? And people
who effortlessly sailed through life, serenely 'virtuous', would they
be properly described as good? They would be harmless: but much
in the way in which the inhabitants of another galaxy are harmless
to us. It is no credit to them: it is just that the laws of physics being
what they are they haven't the remotest chance of affecting us. Likewise, the inhabitants of our alternative cosmos would be precluded,
by the laws of their own psychology, from harming one another.
But praise and blame would not come into it.

6.12 Still, the determinist might not worry at all at this. For, on
his view, praise and blame would have a merely engineering function (3.15), to get people in this world to be a bit better. It would
then be a valuable aspect of that alternative world that there was
no praise and blame to be assigned. The people there would need
no encouragement to 'virtue'.

6.13 But yet we may still have doubts whether such a world would
be more valuable than ours. For as things are, in our cosmos,
morality is a thing which is learnt: it involves effort and the increase
of enlightenment. It is part and parcel of men's strivings. Beings
who are so made that they have to create knowledge, who have, often
painfully, to learn through errors, who have to discover and acquire
skills – such beings are bound to remain imperfect. There are always
goals ahead. But the beings of our imaginary cosmos are, as it
were, too perfect. They come into the world with all that is necessary for complete virtue. They must already be fully enlightened.
It is a static, not an evolving world. Thus, at any rate if we take
the moral and creative struggle seriously, our own cosmos does not
at all seem inferior to theirs. Moreover, as we have seen, it seems
paradoxical to hold that such beings are really free. If we reject the
compatibility between determinism and freedom, then while our
world perchance is a free one, theirs is unfree.

6.14 All this points to an important fact, touched on by Tennant.
You cannot just implant morality or creativity or rationality. As
every teacher knows, there is a great deal of truth in Socrates' idea
that he was a midwife of ideas, helping to bring them to birth for

others. One cannot pump in enlightenment. It can only be elicited from the individual, by guiding him onward and getting him to make his own mistakes. You cannot pump in morality, by a kind of brain-washing; you must get a man to see the good for himself. You cannot produce an artist by thrusting techniques at him: the spark must come from within. So then, there is no question of God simply imposing goodness upon people. In creating free creatures, he is already in a way limiting himself, for thereafter he can no longer play with matter to achieve his ends. No longer can he treat these creatures as he might the galaxies, which can be strung together to order in the sky. Rather, he now must coax and guide. But above all, to a great extent he must leave them to their own devices.

6.15 We therefore see that creativity itself demands the possibility of moral evil. This is not to say that God wills evil as a means to producing creative beings; but it means that this must be accepted as part of the price. Nevertheless, a critic may still reply that even if you can show that this world has more value than our imaginary alternative (together with other similar products of science fiction), might it not be, in some cosmos quite other in character from this one, that persons might be produced who are both perfectly virtuous and free? But this is now a merely bare hypothesis. Would it not at least be reasonable to remain agnostic as to whether this mysterious world of angels were more valuable than our own?

6.16 So far, we have pointed out that an evolutionary, developing world may, for all its sorrows, be more valuable than a static and 'perfect' one. But this at once raises a further problem. If one could still take the myth of Adam literally, and suppose that somehow the whole human race were mysteriously implicated in his fall, one could continue to hold that the possibility might not have been realized. Though this possibility is necessary if there are to be free beings, surely this possibility does not need to be realized. Men might have been good; but instead Adam fell.

6.17 This rather traditional picture, however, cannot be accepted for two reasons. First, we have already pictured free beings as striving, making mistakes, learning through errors. Is it really conceivable that such beings would totally avoid committing moral evil? Is it not implicit in the picture that there was, as it were, bound to be some moral evil? Second, Evolutionary Theory and the researches of archaeologists and anthropologists have made it hard indeed to accept the traditional and Biblical account of the Garden of Eden. It is true that it will probably always remain possible to insert Adam into the gaps in our knowledge of prehistory. But the story has lost its plausibility. Rather the picture is more like this: of men struggling upwards out of barbarism, ignorance and animality. Men have not so suddenly blossomed on the evolutionary tree.

6.18 But if we scrap our literal stories of the Fall, does not this make moral evil in a sort of way inevitable? It is not just that creativity implies the possibility of moral evil: it necessitates it. Only on the soil of evil can good grow. Yet this lands us in a peculiar paradox. Men are responsible, for they are free. But freedom implies that there must be evil. So men are to be blamed for what could not be avoided.

6.19 Of course, we should not here be too much concerned about assigning blame to others. The point is not that we can point an accusing finger at our ancestors. It is more that because of the cruelty, selfishness and other such dispositions inherent in the human condition, men have suffered grievously. Yet we cannot leave the matter there. Maybe much of past cruelty was due to ignorance, unfavourable conditions and so on; so that our ancestors are not so heavily to be blamed. Nevertheless, there is a parallel with the individual's acceptance of responsibility for his past deeds. I accept that I did wrong in the past, even though in a way it was due to my clouded vision rather than an absolutely clear choice of evil. But I see that I could have seen myself more clearly: I could have striven harder for self-knowledge. So I accept my past guilt, and with that already have framed something like a new moral vision for the future. Likewise, and especially because no man is an island (3.57), we must accept the human evils of the past, and thereby see the human condition in a new way. It is not that they, our ancestors,

have been guilty: but *we* have been. Inasmuch as we may feel some
pride in the achievements of the human race in its search for a
better life, so we must see the other side of the coin, and accept the
tragic human failures.

6.20 But here another problem confronts us. So far we have been
discussing the fall of man in the context merely of morality. But
the doctrine always had a deeper religious significance. Does it not
imply that the initial communion between men and God has been
ruptured, and that it required a second Adam to restore this communion? But again, taking the evolutionary picture, it seems unlikely that our remote ancestors, whose life no doubt tended to be
pretty nasty, pretty brutish and pretty short, lived in harmony with
God until a rupture came. It is true that it has been argued, on the
basis of evidence drawn from primitive peoples living today, such as
the Australian aboriginals, that early society believed in a supreme
God, and that this original belief was overlaid by polytheistic and
other cults. But the evidence is hazardous, and it is not very con-
vincing to argue on this basis that God gave a primitive revelation
to man which was obscured and lost because of human wilfulness.
If we reject the hypothesis, then how do we interpret the notion
of a rupture between God and men? If early men had little idea of
the true nature of God, if they were ignorant of the revelation which
later was to culminate in the life and death of Christ, how can they
have turned away from God? For one cannot properly be said
wilfully to ignore or turn one's back upon a person that one does
not recognize.

6.21 We have already argued that knowledge of the divine Being
is not confined just to one tradition. Further, revelation, whether
within the Jewish and Christian traditions, or outside, has been
progressive. Hence, the problem must be solved by reference to
these facts. It is impossible to think of men's having been confronted
in the first instance with a full knowledge of God. Rather, men have
had fragmentary glimpses, no doubt from the beginning, of the
transcendent world, and have in varied ways, some good and some
evil, tried to express this vision. But the greater the knowledge of
God, and the greater human self-knowledge, the greater the sense

of estrangement from God. This sense of estrangement, and of the holiness and glory of the divine Being, is reinforced by the recognition and acceptance of past errors and evils. It is not so much that men have fallen, but that in their slow and painful ascent they have recognized how great the gulf is between God and men. On this view, necessarily, Christ's work is not so much to restore a breach which was earlier wilfully made: it is to create the chance of a deeper communion between men and God than was ever before possible.

6.22 But though all this, it may be objected, is a way of reinterpreting the traditional Christian picture in the light of the evolutionary picture, it still does not answer the problem of evil. First, it has to be shown that creating a theatre for moral and spiritual endeavour was worth all the cruelty and misery. Second, do we not still feel uneasy about the many individual victims of this process? The two points can be distinguished, in that we wish to take a rather quantitative view of the first problem, and not of the second. For it is easy to look upon the first problem as being solved as follows: by pointing out that the sum of human misery, though great, is more than outweighed by the sum of human happiness and achievement and so, on balance, the whole project has been worth while. But this, surely, is too superficial. For one thing, how do we reckon the sum? And, for another, there is the second problem. Is it just that the individual, who may have been tortured or raped or driven mad, should be sacrificed to the greater glory of the human race? Are we to say to him that what matters most is that the race should be capable of marvellous things? You cannot, of course, make omelettes without breaking eggs.

6.23 But it is not eggs, but human beings, of which we are speaking. Is there not a contradiction in saying that, in the interest of the growth of morality and creativity, it may be necessary for individuals to be destroyed? For surely the highest point in morality is to recognize the claims and the worth of the individual. Is not the victim entitled to protest at his being made into a human sacrifice?

6.24 But still: what is the victim really trying to say? If the whole human enterprise is bought at too great a price, because of the victim's personal tragedy, then it would surely have been better if it had never been. Of course, it is too late now to effect this. But suppose the victim had a super-bomb which could painlessly destroy the human race, just by his pressing a button. Would he regard it as right to press that button, to prevent more tragedies?

6.25 Surely, if the victim accepts the whole human enterprise, and failing to press the button would signalize such acceptance, then he is already substituting a new moral attitude for the sense of injustice at his own suffering. It is this: that his torturers really 'know not what they do', that, regarded as representatives of a race which strives, in its freedom, towards great and noble things, they are, as it were, part of that enterprise. Their evil actions themselves, besides paradoxically springing from the nobility of freedom, also teach others the terrible truth of what freedom means. In adopting such an attitude, the victim sees himself as a sacrifice, and a willing one, rather than the petulant accuser of men or of God. It is perhaps therefore of the deepest significance that God himself, if Christian teaching be true, having created beings who, he knew, would in their freedom multiply acts of good and evil, should accept the moral standpoint of the victim. In Christ's sacrifice, there is, as well as the religious act, the moral act of one who sees the human enterprise as good, and yet accepts the evil that comes with it.

6.26 So the substance of the present argument is that the human enterprise, evolutionary and creative as it is, rather than statically 'perfect', may after all constitute the best kind of crown with which the cosmos could be endowed. In creating such a crown, God limits himself and stands a handbreadth off. Thus, though the general pattern of freedom is his handiwork, and though too in intervening in the cruel history of men he co-operates in an intimate way with human creativity, God is not, so to say, the individual author of human events. He did not kill six million Jews: it was we ourselves. If God did it, human freedom becomes meaningless.

6.27 But why should we place so much stress upon the universe as a theatre for *morality*, as though morality were an end in itself?

Surely the point of virtue is that it promotes human welfare and reduces human suffering. Those who stress the intrinsic importance of morality seem to be taking the peculiar view that the happiness and suffering of men are really rather irrelevant and secondary, that what counts is the state of the mind of the torturer rather than the agonized cries of the victim. Thus (so the objection runs) we should distinguish between first-level goods, such as happiness, absence of suffering, etc., and second-level ones, such as courage, temperance and the like. And the point of the second-level goods is that they promote the first-level ones. Thus to see the cosmos as a theatre for the promotion of second-level goods is to get the order wrong. What counts is whether there is welfare, not ultimately as to whether there is virtue.

6.28 One can feel considerable sympathy with this view. For clearly morality does have an important connexion with human welfare. Nevertheless, the objection takes too formalistic a view of morality, and so distinguishes too sharply between the two orders or levels. For morality ultimately centres upon love, the love of humans for one another. This mutual recognition of, and enjoyment of, personal values itself partly springs from the essential freedom and mystery of human beings. This may be something presupposed in the notion that we have duties to one another; but it is also implied more generally in human rationality and creativity. It is, then, not simply that the cosmos provides a theatre for morality. More importantly, because more generally, it provides a theatre for the creation of values. Human welfare, moreover, is not just to be seen in terms of pleasure or happiness or absence of suffering; but also in achievement, in beauty, in understanding, in mutual love. These things may bring happiness; but it would likewise be getting the order wrong if we thought of joys and sorrows as merely 'subjective' states of human beings, and not as occasioned by the realization or failure of human desires and aspirations. The physicist may become depressed by his failure to solve a particular problem. So, then, we should primarily think of the cosmos as a place where it is possible to realize certain values; and this implies among other things that it is a theatre for the creation of morality.

6.29 In the course of the argument so far we have not in any way *established* that this is the best of all possible worlds, or that God is free from blame for the moral evils implicit in human existence. But we have at least made out some sort of general case for saying that perhaps after all the human enterprise is worthwhile, and that maybe an evolutionary and creative world is superior to static perfection. Moreover, though God cannot be held to account for all the particular evils of human history, he has, through his self-sacrifice upon the cross, identified himself with the painful human enterprise, which has already achieved some glories and may in the end rise to sublime heights. But all this, though it suggests an answer to the problem of human evil, does not touch the question of physical evil.

6.30 It is not only that God allows his children to err in the most cruel fashion; but also the cosmos which he has created inflicts upon them the terrors and miseries of earthquakes and cancer, dysentery and crop-failure. Admittedly, some diseases and economic ruins are due to the waywardness of men, and so come under the head of moral evil. But the vast majority of diseases and miseries are produced by the physical world, so often hostile to men. Not only this, but animals too suffer. Admittedly, again, some of this suffering is caused by men: but the immensely greater part of it is nature's work. Everyday, in the scrub and under stones, in jungles and beneath the ocean, bitter unseen strife and painful illnesses are the lot of living creatures. And as we have seen, it is hardly plausible to ascribe all this to a cosmic fall, or to the work of evil spirits. Here, then, is an area where God seems directly responsible for the infliction of suffering.

6.31 This has provided the material for an ingenious contemporary argument, the one already outlined earlier (6.2), to show that religious statements are vacuous or meaningless. For the statement 'God loves his children' seems in meaning straightforward enough. But a human father who loves his children does not inflict suffering upon them gratuitously. And yet, if God is the creator of the cosmos, he inflicts suffering and disease upon human beings. This is counter-evidence to the statement. But the theist (claims the critic), instead of admitting that the empirical evidence tells against his thesis, shifts his meaning. He says 'But God's love is different from human love'. In so doing he is refusing to admit the counter-evidence; but does not realize that thereby he is fatally damaging his own statement. For now 'love' does not mean what it ordinarily means: and by the process of qualifying his original affirmation he is emptying it of such meaning as it might have had. Professor Flew has wittily described this gradual shift of ground as 'death by a thousand qualifications'. He sees this process as typical of religious statements and concludes that by ensuring immunity to falsification theologians have only succeeded in creating a large number of essentially meaningless utterances. All this argument, of course, links up historically with the formulation of the Verification Principle (4.19).

6.32   There are one or two immediate comments to be made. First, the argument draws attention to an ancient difficulty in theology, namely that the theologian wishes to make assertions about a transcendent Being but starts with the language of this world. He therefore is very commonly in the position of having to say, 'Yes, God is a father but not in the ordinary sense'. He is creator, but not just in the way an artist is, and so on. He has to use analogies from ordinary experience, but it is rarely clear how far they are applicable. However, the use of analogies is not confined to theology. In science, for example, words are used in new and extended senses, bearing some analogy to ordinary usage. For instance, a radio-wave is not precisely like a ripple on the surface of a liquid. But here we come to the second comment: at least (it will be said) science has a safe-guard, for the new uses are tied to statements which can be verified or falsified through observation and experiment. But how much check do we have on the statement that God is creator? But we have had occasion to argue earlier (5.51) that the verification and falsification of religious statements, in particular those concerned with a transcendent Being, do not take place through observation, but depend on a variety of factors, including the rather personal and sometimes vague deliverances of intimate religious experience. This will imply in turn that it is less easy to say precisely what religious statements mean: but then this does not at all entail that they have no meaning. Likewise, in music criticism, assertions like 'The second movement has a rich texture' involve analogies which we can understand, and yet which we cannot translate in any precise manner, and cannot verify or falsify simply by observation.

6.33 It should also be noted that the 'death by a thousand qualifications' argument rests on a rather special case, the problem of evil: and it certainly is not to be inferred that because there is some difficulty for the theist here over the empirical evidence, this kind of difficulty extends to religious language in general. For example, the instance could not be used in a discussion of Buddhist language, since the absence there of belief in a creator means that there is no such problem of evil.

6.34 But in any event, is it true that the theist refuses to allow evil as counter-evidence? Perhaps some theologians may have done so: but surely there would be no problem of evil unless already the theist considered that the existence of evil in the cosmos constitutes counter-evidence to belief in a good God. The real question is not: Is this counter-evidence? Rather it is this: Is it overwhelming counter-evidence? Moreover, it is not on the ground that there is suffering in the world that the theist says that God is not literally a father, but on quite other grounds. God is not a father, for he is not the sire of the human race; though he bears some analogy to a father in having created men, and in being there ready to give them guidance, and in having seen to their education.

6.35 We may conclude that, as it stands, the 'death by a thousand qualifications' argument is misdirected. Yet it does add a further spur to us to ask whether the existence of physical evil in the cosmos is really compatible with Christian belief. Can we really conceive that a loving God would have made this malarial and cancerous world?

6.36 An important observation made by Tennant in this connexion is that certainly the cosmos must be governed by regularities. For first, in any event, to be a cosmos at all it must have a pattern (4.49); and second, it is only on the basis of the regularity of things that there can be a rational life. Without regularity, how could there be prediction, or the estimate of probabilities, or prudence? And without these things, how could there be any form of rational behaviour in the world? Without the pattern of consistency in the cosmos, there would then have been no development of men's intellectual powers; and by the same token, no development of morality. In short, a regular background is necessary for the exercise of creativity and freedom. A random and haphazard world, if this can be conceived, could not contain rational and moral beings.

6.37 But then, further, it is exceedingly hard to see how regularities could so be adapted to the changing desires and predicaments of beings, even animals, which display a considerable variation in their behaviour. That is, plasticity of behaviour must characterize conscious beings; but this entails that every so often there must be collisions between these animals and the dumb regularity of the background against which they roam. It is certainly hard to see how accidents and disasters could ever be utterly eliminated from the situation. For example (as Tennant points out) the harmful properties of water – its capacity to drown certain kinds of organisms, for instance – follow from the same source as its beneficial ones. Is it to be suggested that because water sometimes injures, its nature must be made somehow irregular? Suddenly, when a man is drowning, should it turn into air? In this case, apart from the fact that we might thereby collapse the cosmos into a chaos, I could never learn to avoid mistakes, and could not therefore become intelligent. In brief, then, a world which evolves intelligent beings must be a regular world; and yet regularity will mean that disasters to sentient beings will occur.

6.38 This is relevant to a further point. Although we rejected the idea that pain can in detail be justified on the ground of its being useful, a claim that just cannot be substantiated, nevertheless in general it is hard to see how it could be eliminated if there are to be evolving conscious beings.

6.39 Still, despite all this, it will be objected that though perhaps regularities (and therefore collisions with sentient beings) are necessary to the kind of cosmos which we inhabit, and though similarly pain is unavoidable, nevertheless the degree of tragedy and suffering in the actual cosmos is grossly excessive. For instance, could the cosmos not have been constructed without cancer? Or without earthquakes? A father, in educating his son, may have to inflict some pain and discomfort upon him; but a father who gratuitously whipped his boy would rightly be regarded as a monster. It seems then that God can still be charged with wantonness. Or if not that, at least with a kind of bungling which shows that he is not omnipotent and omniscient.

6.40 But how do we decide what is 'excessive' suffering? It is useful to note that if our claim is true, namely that tragedy and suffering cannot be avoided in an ordered cosmos containing conscious beings, then however the world were built, people would still have a problem of evil on their hands: they would still see in the tragedies and miseries evidence against the goodness and power of God. Would they not say: 'Agreed that some of this physical evil is inevitable, but why is there so much? Can we not subtract this bit here, and imagine the world without it? If so, isn't God adding to our suffering in a wanton or bungling way?'

6.41 Suppose too that behind the growth of cancer cells there lay a regularity which was extremely beneficial in other respects. We are again here confronted with the problem of what is theoretically or logically possible (6.11). For if we draw a picture of an alternative cosmos built according to the general pattern of this actual world, then what are we to say if we find that in denying, in our imagination, some feature of the actual world we thereby deny some fundamental regularity of the actual cosmos? Are we not then involving ourselves in a kind of contradiction? But if this is so, then the more science progresses the harder it will be to frame coherent alternative universes built roughly according to the pattern of the real world. If then cancer cells follow from the fundamental properties of matter, it would be hard to wish them away, without also wishing the whole cosmos away.

6.42 It is therefore conceivable that all our evils are in a sense necessary: that is, in general, for the particular accidents and collisions between conscious beings and the regularities of the cosmic background are not totally accountable for in terms of the regularities. But to claim that they are in general necessary is to make a leap of faith: and it can only be an effective one if we are already reasonably convinced that this kind of world in which we have evolved is after all preferable to a statically perfect one. Still, though a leap is needed, this already means that the existence of physical evil is not entirely incompatible with God's goodness and power.

6.43 But, it will still be objected, this general line of argument hinges on the importance of the fact that value and creativity have sprung out of the cosmos. But the way in which this has happened, through the evolution of species, means that animals are made to suffer on behalf of an end-product which they could not conceivably value. Is this not even worse than the cruelties of those regimes who sacrifice the happiness and comfort of a whole generation to produce jam and rockets for the next? It is indeed good that a race which has included Socrates, Leonardo, the Buddha and Einstein should have come into existence. What is morally intolerable is that in order to produce this end-product, millions of animals had to fight and die. This is, of course, a problem chiefly about the higher animals. It is doubtful whether flies can suffer: but monkeys and rats do. Could not God have created, in the *Genesis* manner, all the species more or less at once, without going through the ghastly charade of evolution?

6.44 It is hard to say anything here without seeming callous. And this is another way of admitting that here above all there is strong evidence against God's goodness. One cannot escape by the subterfuge of saying that the animals do not really feel pain. Admittedly, we tend to be too anthropomorphic in our approach to animals, and to ascribe to them the kind of experiences which we ourselves have. And it may well be that animals do not suffer as intensely as we might at first think. But to take the subterfuge seriously would mean that, when we saw a cat lying injured on the road, we could quite justly pass by on the other side. Nor can we have recourse to the Indian doctrine of rebirth and karma. It is true that it provides a general solution to the problem of evil by making suffering the consequence of sin, and by giving the animal a chance of a higher form of life in some future birth. But it is not easy to reconcile with modern biology; and the supposed connexion between suffering and sin is quite speculative.

6.45 It is therefore necessary for the theist to face the issue squarely; and while admitting a considerable degree of bafflement and sorrow, he must rely on the general solution already offered for the existence of physical evil. Certainly, even had there been no rational beings in the cosmos, but only conscious animals such as dogs and monkeys, there would still have been some considerable collision between the regular background and the careers of animals, so that at least some degree of animal suffering would be unavoidable: that is, if there were to be animals at all. Tragedy was already implicit in the creation of the animal kingdom: but nevertheless even here we do not have to see in animals simply a means to the sublimer end of the evolution of human beings. Also there, already, because of the existence among the higher animals of some type of consciousness, there is realized a primitive range of values, brute enjoyments, the sport of the young, the snoozings, and eatings, and prowlings which can, in a sense, make animal life worthwhile.

6.46 Yet there still haunts us the idea that there was another way of arranging things, that ultimately it was unnecessary to evolve rational beings out of a material world, with all the attendant sorrows that that process involves. Especially among religious people this feeling must be strong, since they are inclined to look forward to a sublime (or terrible) future life in another world. If men can live in heaven, enjoying the vision of God, why bother with earth and its struggles and sorrows? If rational beings can exist somehow beyond space and time, why was it necessary to plunge them into a spatio-temporal cosmos? There is a peculiarly powerful tension here in religious thought, since the problem of evil easily tempts people to bring in the next life to redress the balance of this. For instance, it may be believed that though human life is shot through with tragedies, nevertheless in heaven there may be more than adequate compensation. The glories of the beatific vision will far, far out-weigh even the most excruciating cancer. Thus the problem of evil naturally leads us, hopefully, to contemplate the possibility of heaven; and yet this very possibility suggests that God might have rested content with that world and not plunged conscious beings into the maelstrom of this life.

6.47 One traditional answer is to see this life as a kind of moral examination, a spiritual pilgrimage, in which people can earn good marks and bad: if they pass this examination, a life of glory awaits them; but if not, not . . . But this answer already conflicts with important aspects of religious and moral thought. For first, we cannot earn heaven by good works, if Christianity be true; but salvation is the free gift of God. How then can we seriously regard this life as an examination in which there is a prize? Then second, the answer outlined above presupposes that it is just to punish the wicked in hell, everlastingly, even though this could not possibly have any reformatory function. That is, if we believe that the principal aims of punishment are to deter the evil-doer and to reform him, it is hard to see what place in the plan of a good God could be occupied by hell. If, on the other hand, we held a simple retributive theory, that whatever happens, even though the sky fall, it is just and proper that a crime should attract a penalty, we might be happy at the contemplation of hell. But the retributive theory is hard now to maintain (though in a confused way it testifies to something else, namely our feeling that the punishment should fit the crime: a parking offence should not attract hanging, nor should murder result in a trivial fine; in this sense 'an eye for an eye and a tooth for a tooth' is all right as a principle. It is much better than 'an eye for a tooth' (3.15)).

6.48 But we must distinguish between two ideas of heaven that we may have in mind: on the one hand, a statically perfect world having no relation to the actual cosmos, in fact an alternative mode of existence; on the other hand a transcendent state of beings who have evolved in space and time. As to the first idea of heaven, how can we conceive whether such an angelic world would be ultimately better than ours? And even if such a world exists, for angels but not for men, does this mean that God has done wrong to add our world as well? But as to the second idea of heaven, here there can be no problem. If we prize individual existence in heaven, then what we mean by 'individual existence' here must be based on this-worldly ideas. If we say, 'Why couldn't God have put us in heaven straight away?' the answer is simply that we ought to remember what we mean by 'us'. *We* are beings who recognize ourselves as individuals in space and time. There would be no 'us', in the sense in which we use the term, if we had (by way of a contradiction) been put in heaven straight away.

6.49 Our argument so far, then, is that although the existence of evil offers considerable counter-evidence to the goodness and power of God, nevertheless we can sketch out in a general way some conception of how evil can be reconciled with theism. The answer hinges on three main ideas: that the cosmos as it is in a theatre for the creation of values; that the evolutionary way of realizing them may perchance be better than a statically perfect world, and is certainly more intelligible; and that the evolution of values implies a regularity in the cosmos which is liable to come into collision with evolving beings. It should be stressed that this is only a very general sketch; and that it does not establish that this is essentially the best type of cosmos, but it at least makes the faith that it is so less unreasonable than at first sight might appear.

6.50 In thinking of the existence of evil as counter-evidence to theism, we are implicitly assuming that, if it is reasonable to accept theism, the evidence on its behalf must be stronger than this bit of counter-evidence. This already introduces another aspect of the problem which is generally not enough touched upon, though it is discussed by Tennant. It is this: that not merely does God seemingly inflict suffering on his creatures, but thereby powerfully tests the faith of those who believe in him. This is part of the more general question: 'Why is it so hard to believe in God?' That is, God's existence and revelation seem so much wrapped in obscurity and doubt that this already adds a further burden to his creatures.

6.51 It is most vital to discuss this problem, since it is in a way

central to the whole theme of this book. Here we have been considering arguments and objections, evidences and counter-evidences: and
this already indicates that God's existence and nature cannot be
clearly evident. Why is there, if God really does exist, so much
doubt about it? Why should religion embrace so many different
creeds? Why are there various types of religious experience?

6.52   Just as it was useful, in the context of the general problem of
evil, to ask what alternative was being envisaged, so also here. If
God were to reveal himself more clearly, how would he do it?

6.53   Some may not feel the problem, thinking that God has already
clearly revealed himself, through the scriptures. But if one were to
adopt this fundamentalist position, some awkward questions arise.
Why should God in a mysterious and possibly miraculous fashion
have inspired the writers of the Bible to set down his revelation
unerringly? It would surely have been more effective to have written
the Bible in the stars. If the heavens constituted, in their arrange-
ment, a great Bible, how difficult it would be *not* to believe! Or
again, why should the scriptures not grow like vegetables? If our
every cabbage contained holy writ, we would again be unable not
to believe that this was the true revelation. Or again, if God (as we
remarked earlier (2.2)) wished to use miracles as signs of the
authenticity of Christ's teaching, surely something more spectacular
could have been performed. Such questions can easily be multiplied;
and yet they have rather an unconvincing ring – for they seem to get
the point and nature of revelation all wrong. But it is as well to see
just why they get it wrong, for this will in part solve our problems
about the difficulty of faith.

6.54   The first comment is one which we have made before (2.2):
namely that here revelation is wrongly and too mechanically conceived as the utterance of a string of propositions. Rather, behind
the scriptural writings, lie religious experience and historical events.
It is in these that God reveals himself. Let us take these points
separately.

6.55   We may ask a similar sceptical question about religious experience. If God wishes to make himself known then why are not experiences such as that of St Paul on the Damascus Road more common, or even universal? One reason, as we have noted (5.40), no doubt is that the way which God has chosen – the way of freedom and creativity – precludes him from forcing himself upon men. It was perhaps because St Paul, through his earlier hate against Christ, already betrayed a kind of love for him, that he was one to whom Christ could show himself in such a way. Moreover – and we shall come to this in a moment – historical events, such as those momentous ones, surrounding St Paul's conversion, do not recur nor are they stereotypes. Finally, as we have seen (5.39), the obscurity of God's self-revelation must be bound up with his transcendence of the cosmos. Having created an independent and orderly universe, he is necessarily limited in the possibility of his intervention. That there can be an element of randomness and irregularity is possible: but that the regularities should be overwhelmed by God's interventions would mean the destruction of the cosmos and thereby of the whole creative enterprise which God had undertaken. At the same time the divine transcendence involves that to us he is and must be in some measure mysterious and incomprehensible. Though we should try to make his ways plain, so far as this is possible, we cannot hope for complete success.

6.56 No doubt we may dream that it would be nice if the truth about God were handed to us on a plate, so that the whole business could be dealt with and finished with. But this dream is inconsistent with the evolutionary character of the cosmos, and with the nature of knowledge. Knowledge comes through the process of learning, but not in parrot-fashion. It is illusory to suppose that there could be any genuine knowledge of spiritual or moral matters which was imposed upon us or dictated to us.

6.57 Similarly, in regard to the rather obscure historical events in which God has revealed himself, what alternative are we hankering after? Perhaps, we may think, it would have been better if Jesus had lived in the era of the film and of the tape-recorder. Think how many Biblical scholars would be put out of business. Think how much more we would know about him! But yet much doubt and uncertainty about him would still remain. More fundamentally, if God reveals himself thus in history, there is bound to be a scandal of particularity, a scandal that Jesus should appear there and then and not here and now. In any event, the might-have-beens of history are incredibly hard to evaluate. If God had waited for the tape-recorder he might have waited in vain.

6.58 So then it seems to be in the nature of the case that religious truth must have rather obscure and tricky evidences. And since we are dealing with the transcendent, which cannot be observed (2.42), it is not surprising that there should be variations in dogma and in the interpretation of experience. This kind of conclusion about the nature of religious thought and language is, in a sense, what the philosophy of religion is ultimately about. The examination of arguments and evidences is important in its own right; but it also throws light on the nature of religion. This makes for philosophical clarity; for it is the mark of the unphilosophical person to fail to see distinctions where they exist (to think of art-criticism as though it is quite simply on a par with, say, science; to treat moral rules as if they were observational facts, and so on). Thus in attempting to solve the problem about faith, which arises from the more general problem of evil, we are recapitulating the whole argument of this book.

6.59 In brief, the truth of religion may still stand despite the counter-evidences which evil presents, because of the very nature of religious truth.

7

Wittgenstein, Death and the Last Judgment

7.1 I T is less fashionable nowadays among philosophers of religion to attempt to provide grounds for the immortality of the soul than it once was. Nevertheless, the question of the focus of religious hope (and fear) remains important. We have already touched on the topic of heavenly existence in the discussion of the problem of evil (6.46ff.). But how is meaning to be assigned to belief in such a state? Can survival of death and a Last Judgment be conceived? It is useful to connect the discussion of this to some remarks of Wittgenstein on these topics.

7.2 Wittgenstein's profound effect upon modern philosophy has occurred paradoxically in two phases – paradoxically because the later Wittgenstein of, for instance, the *Philosophical Investigations* held views about language and meaning radically different from those presented in the *Tractatus Logico-Philosophicus*. The business of Wittgensteinian exegesis is difficult, not only because of the shifting nature of his views and the aphoristic style which he adopted, but also because of his tendency towards the esoteric. Painfully concerned that his thoughts should not be misrepresented and vulgarized, he tended to confine his teaching to an inner circle of disciples. However, I am not so much concerned here with the correct interpretation of, say, the *Tractatus*, but rather with the effect it has had upon philosophy – with the way, that is, in which it has often been interpreted. The earlier Wittgenstein held a theory of meaning which seemed close to that of what came to be known as Logical Positivism, as expounded, e.g., by A. J. Ayer (4.19). A proposition has meaning if and only if we know what would verify it; it must be 'compared with reality'. Certainly the Logical Positivists claimed a partly Wittgensteinian ancestry. However, it is doubtful whether Wittgenstein himself meant that verification is necessarily only through sense-experience. Given this restriction, however, the criterion of meaning certainly appears to render meaningless statements about God, etc., lying 'beyond' the world of sense-experience; and certainly too Wittgenstein himself took talk about God, etc., as transcending reality to be meaningless, or belonging to the realm of what cannot be said. The major difficulty about the *Tractatus* is knowing what Wittgenstein meant by the 'world' or 'reality'. Why, for instance, should it be assumed that God does not reveal himself *in* the world, that he is not part of what 'is the case'? And why, mysteriously, should Wittgenstein have appeared to have connected the concept of the world with individual experience, in his tantalizingly obscure remark: 'As in death, too, the world does not change, but ceases. Death is not an event in life. Death is not lived through.'?

7.3 One thought which may have been behind Wittgenstein's banishment of God to the realm of the unutterable, beyond the world of all that 'is the case', is the old doctrine of God's necessity. What is the case, within certain restrictions posed by Wittgenstein's theory of meaning, is contingently so. But God is not contingent. We have already looked sufficiently at this problem (4.4ff.). Another reason may have been the recognition that the concept *God* has to do with values, with what ought to be the case rather than what is the case; in his early period, Wittgenstein seemed to think that ethics is transcendental, and concerned with what goes beyond reality. About this, however, there ought to be no great mystery. If I ought to do something and yet do not do it, the world has one pattern; if I do it, on the other hand, it has another. Ideals which do not operate are not part of reality, except in so far as they exist in the thoughts of individuals. Ideals which do operate exhibit a connection between human thoughts and emotions on the one hand and another aspect of the world on the other.

7.4 The notion that the world ceases at death implies much about Wittgenstein's idea of the world. This in part stemmed from his theory of language. Unwilling to interpose a metaphysical entity, namely the proposition, between words and reality, he considered (in the days of the *Tractatus*) that the names which are used to refer to objects in the world do so partly in virtue of the intention of the user. The glue which sticks the name to the object is the intention of the user of the name that it should refer to the object. This is only one condition of the application of Wittgenstein's picture theory of meaning, according to which language mirrors reality in such a way that the limits of reality coincide with the limits of what can be said: it is only one, and yet it is one. If so, the disappearance of the user of language, by death, involves the cessation of the world. Admittedly, there are questions, about what counts as death, and whether the death of the body is the same as the death of the individual: to these questions we shall come. But evidently Wittgenstein, in his early period, considered death as such that it wiped out the world. Given his theory of language, this was intelligible.

7.5 Yet we all know that when I die the world will go on. It is neither dependent on my consciousness, nor upon my language-using. It is not even dependent on *us* (i.e. consciousnesses or language-users in the plural). Perhaps in a way Wittgenstein was right to say that the world does not change, by death. But how could it genuinely *cease*?

7.6 Hitherto, in the arguments that have been deployed in this book about the world, etc., we have been thinking of the cosmos as something which could exist whether or not human beings did. There is, however, another sense, as when we talk about the world of Paul Slickey. Here we think of the world in relation to an individual – his world. This 'existential world' certainly ceases when he ceases. The philosophical realist, however, is liable to distrust such a world; since his world conforms to the 'objective' idea of the universe, which would go on existing even if I or we did not.

7.7 It happens that Wittgenstein's cryptic remark about death has been expanded by W. H. Poteat in an interesting and important article, 'I will Die', which follows on from one on 'Birth, Suicide and the Doctrine of Creation' (both reprinted in D. Z. Phillips, ed., *Religion and Understanding*). Poteat makes much use of the distinction between the objective and what I have called the 'existential' worlds. The former is in principle describable without the use of personal pronouns ('I', 'we', 'you', etc.); it would, so to say, be the realm of 'it', 'this', 'those', etc. By contrast the 'existential' world is *my* world. It is mine in the sense that 'I have a relation to the body, its behaviour and the environment of its actions (which is the world *for me*), which is part of what I mean by "I", that can never be identical with the relation which *you* have, and that cannot be expressed in the language lacking the first personal pronoun singular' (p. 132). It follows from the distinction made by Poteat that the expression 'I will die' cannot be exhaustively analysed into a purely third person reading of 'This body will undergo a radical change, including ceasing to behave in certain ways, etc.' *My* world does not change at death; it ceases.

7.8 Poteat, of course, is not arguing that the dissolution of the body is not part of what is involved in the assertion 'I will die'. I am surely in part predicting a change which will occur in the 'objective' world of commonsense; but what I am saying is not *just* about that world. There is an asymmetry between 'I will die' and 'Jones will die' (said about someone else); for in saying the latter I am describing an event in the world; but I am not in the world as Jones is in the world. That is, I am not in my existential world as an object of experience, etc., since it is the special relationship between me and my body, etc., which defines my world, and that relationship does not apply to other bodies, etc.

7.9 Much depends, in this account, on Poteat's view of the relation between 'I' language and behavioural language, i.e. reports of bodily behaviour, etc. According to this view, the first person pronoun includes reference to bodily behaviour, etc., but its reference is not thereby exhausted. But this does not entail that the self is a ghostly substance or thing – for that too in principle is describable in 'objective' world terms; and indeed would have to be, for the idea of a thing has to be cashed in empirical language. Thus the idea that I might survive death is ruled out. *Either* one simply identifies me with bodily behaviour, etc.; in which case it is contradictory to say that after it ceases I still exist – *or*, in accordance with the Poteat view of 'I', one is asserting the existence of an 'I' constituted both by bodily behaviour and something more; in which case the use of 'exists' is ruled out, because what counts as existing or not existing does so only in the context of empirical language.

7.10 Hence, language is put under a peculiar strain when we seriously say 'I will die'. Even to say 'After I die there will be nothing' is not to speak in terms of the objective world. When language is thus subject to pressure, according to Poteat, it gives rise to the use of myth. Myth is anchored to the empirical, for it is about my existential reality; but it is not literally about it. Its non-literalness helps to convey the 'something more' than the empirical implied in talk of my death. Thus the central Christian myth about death is that of the Resurrection of the Body, which ties the individual firmly to his historical (bodily) acts; and which points to the involvement of the person in fellowship with God. The myth of the Resurrection then is a way of the Christian's saying that he will have fellowship with God (yet 'at the end of history' – here another mythic, eschatological idea is used). However, though the pressure on language gives rise to the use of mythic language, it does not follow that this is simply invented (indeed the Christian myth is 'given').

7.11 Before passing on to criticize certain aspects of Poteat's view, let us note that it has a certain analogy to the picture drawn by the early Wittgenstein. The 'objective' world of Poteat (with the personal pronouns taken out) is not unlike the world of 'all that is the case' whose formal structure Wittgenstein attempted to trace in the *Tractatus*. But in place of the mystical, the ineffable, which could show itself but not be delineated in propositions, Poteat substitutes the mythic. Through this oblique use of language, something is said about what, so to say, lies beyond the empirical, 'objective', world.

7.12 Since Poteat has described the objective world from a linguistic point of view (knocking out the personal pronouns), his characterization of it can in no wise determine the stuff of which that objective world is made (any more than Wittgenstein's account of the world, which is purely logical and formal, can determine what the constituents of the world are). Yet there is implicit in his account a certain view of what constitutes the empirical; in particular the empirical aspect of the person seems to be made up of bodily behaviour, or of the body and its animated behaviour. The cessation of the latter entails the death of the person. He does mention, but by implication rejects, the Platonic notion of an embodied soul, which can persist after death (though he treats this primarily as a mythic picture, an alternative to the Christian myth of the Resurrection of the Body). However, it is as well to explore the alternative models which might be set up, in such a way that death might only mean 'bodily death' or 'the death of this body'; or alternatively that one can distinguish between $death_1$ (bodily death) and $death_2$ (the cessation of the individual). For if Poteat's argument holds, it holds in virtue of his using the second concept of death, though he makes it appear to hold in virtue of the first concept. Thus when he points out that 'I have died' makes no sense or has no use, he is right in relation to $death_2$; but not at all obviously right in relation to $death_1$.

7.13   To exhibit this point further, let us notice a certain ambiguity in the concept of the body. Supposing I say, 'There was firing in the streets and bodies were lying everywhere', I would be taken to refer to human bodies as they actually are (though dead, no longer animated, their behaviour gone). This ordinary concept of a human body refers to something typically being five or six feet tall, with two eyes, ears, arms, legs, hair only in parts, etc. $Death_1$ then means the death of the ordinary body. But the concept of the individual or person need not (perhaps is not) tied so closely to the ordinary human body. For instance, we can conceive (as in science fiction) that we meet Martians, who are persons, but their bodies have three eyes and are a hundred feet tall, etc. We can easily speak about $death_1$ in relation to Martians; so that now the concept is extended not to mean the death of the ordinary body but the death of the body of the person in question (different sorts of persons have different sorts of bodies). Now it might be argued that a person has to have some sort of body or other, i.e. that the concept of a totally disembodied person is self-contradictory. To this point we shall come shortly. But if we accept this thesis for the moment, it is still possible to construct a notion of the individual such that his death does not coincide with the death of the ordinary human body (or of the ordinary Martian body). For instance, the destruction of the ordinary body could give rise to a miasmic 'subtle' body, through which the individual continues to express himself. This indeed is a common theme in some religious folk-lore. However, some conditions have to be met if we are to be satisfied that such a 'miasmic' individual is *the same person as* the previously ordinarily embodied person.

7.14 Normally we assume, in identifying someone as the same person as we met last year on holiday, that the individual's body has continued, is the same body; but suppose he is in heavy disguise. We do not recognize him by his bodily characteristics; but it might be that he lets slip some information that only he could have known, or we recognize him by his handwriting. Let us call the former basis of recognition a 'sign of biographical uniqueness' and the second 'sameness of style'. Such bases of recognition could easily be conceived to apply to a miasmic individual. But a condition of this at least is that there is some communication or transaction between the recognizer and the miasmic individual. Thus first, the idea of the continuity of the individual with a miasmic body is easily conceivable; and second, the question of whether in fact such survival after ordinary bodily death occurs is to be settled empirically (it is a question of whether there are reports of transactions with such *post mortem* persons, and whether these reports are well-founded). Do embodied persons (in the ordinary sense of 'body') ever encounter such miasmic individuals? It might not have much relevance for religion, for at one level all that would be shown by the existence of miasmic survival is that all or some people live longer than we had imagined (but we tend to live longer than our eighteenth-century ancestors). Still, given that by death we mean the cessation of the ordinary body, the conceivability of miasmic survival indicates a use for 'I have died'.

7.15 The idea of miasmic survival stretches our current concept of the person, perhaps; for it stretches the notion of embodiment. How far can the stretching go without breaking up the concept of the person? For instance, does belief in reincarnation or rebirth make proper sense? Here it is not a question of the *mythic* possibility of the picture of reincarnation (that doubtless is conceded by Poteat; and as we shall see there is no bar to the meaningfulness of the idea from the standpoint of the later Wittgenstein). The question is as to its literal possibility: could our commonsense concept of the person be so stretched as to make rebirth intelligible? In principle, it seems that it could; since if I can die in my present body but continue in a miasmic body, there is no reason why the miasmic body should not then die and be succeeded by a further body, perhaps somewhat resembling its predecessor though very different from my present body. One could have grounds for holding A to be the same individual as B, and B to be the same individual as C, without directly having grounds for holding that A is identical with C.

7.16 It seems, then, that the claim that death is not an event in life, and Poteat's affirmation of the self-contradictory nature of empirical survival of death, are not simply conceptual theses. For them to be conceptual truths they would have to be about death$_2$; but the identification of death$_2$ with ordinary bodily death (what we usually mean by death) is an empirical one. Or putting the matter differently, from another angle, the definition of the world through 'it' language does not prescribe its actual nature; to speak of the language describing the world in this way as 'empirical' language conceals an ambiguity. It may be empirical because there are objective methods of verification, etc.; but secretly 'empirical' is being identified with what contingently is (or is taken to be) the case. Since we believe that death is the end of the individual, we define it to be so. That is, we define death in terms of ordinary bodily dissolution. But it in no way follows that this belief represents a special way of using language, namely empirically.

7.17 However, another aspect of Poteat's thesis seems definitely conceptual, his rejection of a substantive thing-like account of the self. The introduction of the first personal pronoun does not, so to say, add to the empirical facts making up the world; but it radically changes the way in which the world is viewed. He writes: 'When I use "I" of myself, something is being named which is *for me* not just the spatio-temporal speaker or behaver from which the noise "I" has come. If you ask me what it is that is named, hoping for an answer given in reports of behaviour alone, then of course I can't say . . . If you do not ask me what it is that is named *in these terms*, then my answer is quite simple: myself!' There is, however, a problem about what is meant by 'behaviour'. Typically, it means the ways I express myself through my body, but does not include many activities internal to my body (such as the operation of my brain-cells). It also does not usually include a whole range of mental states. Thus if I say 'You could not tell from his behaviour what he was thinking' there is an implied distinction between his outer behaviour and some mental process. As we saw in an earlier chapter (3.34), there are reasons to maintain the distinction between mental and physical states, etc. Does Poteat's concept of behaviour include mental states as well? It needs to, for certainly it is a fact about the world that I am thinking about Waterloo (if I am) and one which is reportable. Of course some mental activities are necessarily connected with behaviour – such as writing up the results of an experiment or doing a jigsaw puzzle; others, however, are not so analytically connected with sorts of behaviour, such as remembering that evening in Caserta or doing sums in one's head. We may call these 'non-behavioural mental activities'. Given Poteat's account, he would have to say that 'I' refers to mental activities and bodily behaviour, etc., plus *something more*, such that the something more cannot be described in terms of mental activities, bodily behaviour, etc. It cannot even be described in terms of non-behavioural mental activities. However, it is worth asking whether it would not be possible for non-behavioural mental activities to function in which the body functioned in the previous argument. That is, can we conceive the self as such that 'I' refers to non-behavioural mental activities plus something more? More crudely: could the disembodied mind do the same job as the body, or as the embodied mind?

7.18 In one way obviously it couldn't, for as things are what I *mean* when I refer to myself includes my body. Further, my non-behavioural mental activities are mere fragments in the stream of my autobiography. It would indeed be odd to write the story of my life and only include disconnected recollections and sums in the head. But we can still ask: suppose bodily behaviour ceases, at what we call death, could there still be a use for 'I', such that it refers to a two-phase person, the first phase being embodied, the second consisting in non-behavioural mental events which are continuous with the biographical events of the first phase? The second-phase life would at first seem rather thin and unattractive, though intellectuals would probably find it richer than others. From the religious point of view there would be no reason why it should not involve communion with or an inner vision of God. The supposition does not seem contradictory. But could it be an empirical hypothesis, like that of the miasmic individual? A disembodied individual would be incapable of communication, of entering into transactions with others, it would seem. However, with a bit of ingenuity one can imagine ways in which two such individuals might learn to communicate (if for instance one's thoughts were deliberate, except for some, which give a coherent account of a different biography from one's own, then one would have grounds for thinking that someone else was communicating). Under such circumstances, the disembodied minds would themselves take on the characteristics of bodies, though made of a different 'stuff' from usual; since they would be capable of having effects on other minds. Thus so far the new hypothesis turns out to be a refined version of that about the miasmic individual. Let us call the second phases of such individuals their 'mental bodies': or rather they are now persons with mental bodies.

7.19 Does it now make sense to suppose that they could survive the death of their *mental bodies*? We would have to specify what was meant by 'death' here. In the case of bodily death, what is meant is that the body ceases finally to function, in such a way that it will no longer exhibit behaviour. Even if the person might live on in another body, it has indeed to be another body. The supposition depends on being able to identify a body, and the criteria of sameness have to do with spatio-temporal continuity, etc. But what would the replacement of one mental body by another mental body amount to? What are the criteria for identifying a given mental body? It seems that all we can do is point to biographical coherence. If this is so then it surely makes no sense to suppose that a person can be re-embodied in a different mental body, since this would *ex hypothesi* be biographically incoherent. Can it be me any more when I look back not on my life but Napoleon's? (When 'I' look back on Napoleon's!) This incidentally is one of the major difficulties about belief in reincarnation – trying to see the biographical coherence between my life and the preceding lives I am supposed to have led. We may conclude, then, that a sense can be given to the idea of mental-bodily survival; but that of course there could be no survival of mental-bodily death. But presumably there still remains the theoretical possibility that there might be no mental-bodily death (that is, one could go on existing for ever in a mental-bodily fashion).

7.20 Though so far we have been considering the 'I' as referring to the body (whether physical, mental or both) plus something more; but such that the something more can be regarded as a thing added to the body, etc., it is worthwhile briefly exploring the possibility of treating it as referring to a transcendental ego, or self lying beyond or behind mental and physical states. Let us call this the idea of a 'pure soul'. Sometimes it is imagined that somehow upon mental and physical death the pure soul survives. What significance would there be in this? As a person, I express myself through my body, have a certain sort of body, a certain character, and individual style of doing things, certain fears, desires, ideals and so on. But on the hypothesis now being considered, the pure soul lies behind or beyond all these elements in my personhood. This being so, it is hard to understand how the survival of such an entity would in any way amount to *my* survival. It would be as if the gravedigger took out a gold filling from one of my teeth, and kept it: the gold filling would, so to say, live on, even after I am gone; but because it has none of my fears, wishes, memories or quirks it would in no sense be me living on.

7.21 How is it then that the idea of a pure soul is prevalent in some religions, above all in some Indian religions? Appearances are deceptive: the soul there is not quite a pure soul – for it is in principle an object of experience. In the interior vision, one can attain a non-dual experience of the soul, giving one insight into its difference from the natural world and liberation from sorrow, etc. The idea of the soul has a positive role to play in the form of life represented in such religions – to this point we shall return, in considering the later Wittgenstein (7.25).

7.22 But taken merely metaphysically the pure soul is a useless and superfluous entity, and in no way explains personal continuity. But does it fare any worse than the 'something more' which however cannot be described in empirical terms and to which 'I' in part refers, according to Poteat? It does, in so far as the 'I' of Poteat necessarily also refers to some kind of body, so there could be no question of a disembodied 'I' in the way we are now trying to conceive a disembodied soul. Nevertheless, Poteat's 'I' is connected with the mythic use of language. But the use of such language is opaque. For instance, the idea of the Resurrection of the Body connects with fellowship with God. But what does the 'will' amount to in saying that 'I will have fellowship with God (at the end of history)'? This seemingly cannot be cashed in terms of a future empirical event. It cannot relate to my survival of death. Why then the future tense?

7.23 It might be possible to get some light on these matters by considering the approach to religious discourse found in the later Wittgenstein. The sea-change which came over Wittgenstein between the *Tractatus* and the *Philosophical Investigations* was this. Whereas in the *Tractatus* he employed a largely theoretical and formal account of meaning, in the later work he took a realistic look at the way language actually works. In the former work he employed the picture theory of meaning in which propositional signs mirror the structure of reality (though not without the intervention of a mental act, namely the intention of the speaker), and which compelled him to think that a term could not have meaning unless there was some perfectly determinate object or objects which it named; but in the latter work, he was concerned with various uses to which language is actually put. The different sets of uses are what Wittgenstein calls 'language-games'. The speaking of language is part of an activity or of a form of life. Thus, e.g., the meaning and point of moral utterances cannot be understood without reference to its living milieu, namely in the taking of certain sorts of decisions, of acquiring certain sorts of attitudes, and so on. The assumption in this later phases is that there is a whole host of language-games, and that many philosophical errors arise through trying to force them in to a single frame (precisely what Wittgenstein had attempted in effect in the *Tractatus*).

7.24   The application of all this to religion is this: that religious language itself is a special language-game or set of language-games, going with a special form or forms of life. The pluralism of the latter Wittgenstein reacts against the empiricist attempt at a monism in which religious language, because not conforming to verificationist criteria of meaning, is banished as senseless. Wittgenstein did not say a great deal about the actual nature of religious language and belief as he understood them. Most of what he did say is contained in the *Lectures and Conversations on Aesthetics, Psychology and Religious Belief* (these are records by students, rather than Wittgenstein's *ipsissima verba*, but there is little doubt of their substantial accuracy in conveying his thoughts on these topics).

7.25   One of the instances of belief which he considers there is belief in a Last Judgment (also belief in the Resurrection of the Body). What is the difference between the man who believes in the Last Judgment and the man who does not? It is not a matter of empirical evidence, since belief that some peculiar events will occur in a thousand years' time does not by itself amount to religious belief, while the religious believer may not, and may know that he does not, have much if anything in the way of recognizable empirical evidence for his belief. Thus the disagreement can scarcely be treated as a case of the one man believing the opposite of what the other man does. Believing the opposite might occur in such a context as this: one man thinks that the Third World War is likely to break out because of events in Czechoslovakia and another denies the likelihood (he has a different estimate of the evidence, etc.). Wittgenstein by the same token does not want to say that the believer's conviction is unreasonable (a term of disapprobation): it is not playing in the same league as beliefs which we might term reasonable or unreasonable. A man who has such a belief has a certain picture, e.g. of the Last Judgment, and this picture has its meaning and point partly in virtue of there being a technique for using it, which has to be learned, and partly in virtue of the way in which it regulates his life. As to the former aspect: Wittgenstein uses the illustration of talk about the eye of God; it is sharp enough to count the hairs on a man's head, but the question 'Does God have bushy eyebrows?' is absurd. Thus the meaning of the picture 'the eye of God' depends on how people go to use it, the consequences they draw, etc. The meaning is not perspicuous from the phrase itself.

7.26 The difference, then, between the believer and the non-believer is not a matter of the latter's believing the opposite: but of the believer's having a picture and the non-believer not having it. The having of the picture has to do with its regulative effect upon a person's life. Since having a picture cannot be reduced to an empirical belief, it seems to play a function similar to the notion of myth in Poteat. The latter also seems to suppose that there could not be reasons for preferring one picture or myth to another.

7.27 How does this account relate to the empirical possibilities of survival which we considered earlier? Would it be possible to say: use the picture of the immortality of the soul or of the Resurrection of the Body, but do not think that *actually* you will survive or that actually your body will be reconstituted? Or: use the picture of the eye of God, but do not suppose that God actually exists? One answer to such questions might be that they are wrongly posed. That is, what it means to say that I actually exist after death is constituted by the picture; what it means to say that God exists is constituted by the set of pictures used.

7.28 Although there is some substance in this mode of rebutting the questions – since religious belief is not the same as scientific beliefs, etc., and since certainly analogies or pictures are used in explicating the idea of God – the rebuttal is not altogether satisfactory. Consider, for instance, the fear of hell. A sulphurous picture is presented, and connected with specified sorts of sin. A man's belief in this picture is seen in the terror with which he lives, induced in part by his load of guilt. It surely makes a difference if he recognizes that from an empirical point of view there is no ground for belief in survival, and that his sufferings will cease with his death. For however much we may want to say that belief in hell is a matter of keeping before one a certain picture, this cannot exclude us from considering questions of survival at the empirical level. The difference that the recognition of his literal non-survival would make is this: that his terror is no longer like that which a person might have if he were told that on a certain date the police would begin to torture him. The latter case of terror is normal, and in a straightforward way rational. But terror at a non-literal hell is transformed into something different: it is a vivid realization, *sub specie aeternitatis*, of one's guilt, and of one's sense of alienation from God. If a man in these circumstances nevertheless sometimes began to fear hell the way he would fear torture, ought he not to be reassured?

7.29 Wittgenstein remarked that the attempt to establish religious belief scientifically turned it into superstition; by analogy it might be thought that belief in empirical survival (e.g. in hell) is superstitious. But it surely cannot be held that the presence of literal empirical beliefs makes a religion superstitious. For instance, Christ's death on the cross is an historical event, to be established, in principle, empirically. Further, the criteria of what counts as superstition have to do with the criteria of truth in religion; and it is possible that the truth is that people do survive, etc., beyond death. However, superstition also has to do with attitudes. From the point of view of a religion of grace such as Christianity, the attempts to manipulate the divine, to use the sacraments magically, etc., count as superstition; and these attempts rest upon a certain attitude. We should therefore ask what motives people may have for belief in survival; for it might turn out that these are such as to show that some kinds of survival are not relevant to the heart of religion.

7.30   One obvious motive is the desire to live longer. After all, a man who is seriously ill is not to be blamed if he wishes to pull through and carry on living a bit longer. Why not wish for a bit more after bodily death? However, such a desire for prolongation of life is not fundamentally relevant to religion; and if some folk do have a miasmic or mental existence for a few years beyond death, this is quite analogous to the fact that some folk live to ninety, rather than the regulation seventy. Such a hypothesis does not alter the fundamental framework of life. Paradoxically it would be more relevant to science than to religion, since it would open up new problems in psychology and biology.

7.31   Another motive is the desire to see loved ones again beyond the grave. But suppose there were re-death beyond the grave? Would the same demand be made? And so on *ad infinitum*? Such a desire for boundless union with those dear to us itself indicates a boundless love. If that really existed here and now, it would not be affected by death; it would be immune to contingencies. Still, as well as the love there is its expression and enjoyment: to love a person implies wanting to be with him or her, do things together, etc. Is it then that the desire to survive is the desire to do more things together than this life has contingently made possible? If so, the case is rather analogous to that described in the previous paragraph. Again, it does not fundamentally alter the framework of life. Sometimes a spouse dies on the honeymoon; but for many, married love extends a long time.

7.32   Another motive is the desire to see justice done. Those who suffer in this life can gain compensation in the glorious next life. (The evil too may be punished.) We have already touched on this topic in the previous chapter. Given that we are thinking about the fate of others, it presents a curious picture of the operations of God, producing a world in which there are tragedies, but wiping them out in the next. However, let us consider how the matter looks autobiographically. I suffer: do I then look for future happiness which will make up for my tribulations? If I connect this future bonus with the activity of God, then is it just a hope? For instance, I think that if I'm knocked down in the street someone will come along to take me to hospital, repair my injuries and so on. It is good of the State to organize such services. But how can I have assurance that God will organize likewise a future life for me? If I rely upon a real knowledge of his character, then I have already entered into some close fellowship with him. In these circumstances, do I not already have the peace of God, which suffering will not take away from me? Well, it could be that I rely so to speak on hearsay, on the testimony of saints: though I do not have that peace, others have had it. But this does not alter the situation essentially – for the saint who has found the peace of God would only begin to think of God's providing heavenly life for those who do not have that peace as the provision of a milieu of fellowship with God – a place for that kind of peace. In brief, the ground which anyone might have for belief in a life of peace beyond the present suffering connects directly with fellowship and communion with God.

7.33 In this case the motive for survival is directly religious, although it is paradoxical: in that those who already have the peace of God would feel no special call to long for a personal survival in which suffering is made up for by the provision of countervailing joys. Interestingly and conversely, belief in a hell in which other folk are punished is scarcely loving: and the only person who could have a loving motive for belief in hell is one who is himself willing to go to hell if he alienates himself from God.

7.34 The correct motive, then, for belief in an afterlife, from the religious point of view and within the context of theism, depends directly on fellowship with God. But can we say that belief in God is sufficient ground for an accompanying belief in heaven or of the Resurrection of the Body?

7.35 As we have seen, there are certain types of survival, e.g. miasmically or in mental bodies, which can be delineated, apparently without self-contradiction, and the truth of which could be in principle established empirically. I do not want to enter here into a review of the evidence in favour of spiritualism, etc.; it does no harm to keep an open mind – it may be that miasmic or mental existence does persist beyond what we ordinarily consider to be bodily death. But this empirical hypothesis is neither well established nor directly relevant to religious concerns. It is perhaps relevant just in the way in which the topography of Brazil is relevant: knowing it is a condition of solving some of the living problems of the country and the people. But one does not get to know of the topography of Brazil by praying or by reading the Bible. For this kind of survival it would seem that belief in God would not be a good ground.

7.36 If there is some future aspect of eternal life belief in which rests on fellowship with God, its form must correspond to the ground on which it is affirmed. As we saw, this was the desire that we might have the peace of God beyond the grave, even though paradoxically those having the best insight into God's nature would already possess that peace. We might put the matter as follows: that there is the hope of fellowship with God in the nearer presence of God, i.e. in the transcendent sphere which he occupies. Would it be possible for us somehow to be recreated in that nearer presence?

7.37 If we can make dim sense of this idea, it is only because we can already make some sense of the concept of God. Whether such a recreation in heaven does or does not involve an incoherence or contradiction – about this we can at best be agnostic. So it seems that after all we are left with the opacity of the myth or picture. However, it does not at all follow from this that the picture-analysis of religious belief is comprehensively satisfactory, or that religious belief is, so to say, beyond what is either reasonable or unreasonable. For the ground upon which a believer might rest his opaque hope in his recreation in the presence of God is belief in God. And as we have seen in the foregoing chapters, belief in God raises questions of religious and other reasoning which cannot be escaped. By the same token, Poteat is wrong to think that there could be no grounds for preferring one eschatology to another. And if this is so,

Wittgenstein cannot be correct in thinking that the atheist and the believer do not in some sense believe the opposite.

7.38 Wittgenstein's rather fragmentary account of religious belief appears correct both in his emphasis upon the connection of concepts with forms of life and in his implied pluralism: religious concepts are not to be assimilated to scientific ones, etc. But it appears to neglect the necessity for a bipolar treatment of picture and myth. The meaning of a picture, such as the Last Judgment, is in one direction tied to the pole of biography, human practices, morality. But in another direction it is tied to the pole of the transcendent. It is the former tie-up which is emphasized by both Wittgenstein and Poteat; but it is only by connecting the myth of the Last Judgment or the Resurrection of the Body with belief in a God with whom one could enter into fellowship that it escapes being merely a picture or regulative device. Further, as we have seen, Wittgenstein is over-irrationalistic in his presentation of the nature of religious belief.

7.39 This is brought out by his remark '. . . you don't get in religious controversies, the form of controversy where one person is *sure* of the thing, and the other says: "Well, possibly".' Though religious beliefs are different from other beliefs, they are not insulated from them, nor are they insulated from one another. This indeed is one reason why belief in souls has faded, and why distinctions between religious beliefs and other sorts are made now with more clarity. For religious beliefs abut on non-religious ones (e.g. moral ones), and changing knowledge of the world has an effect upon religious beliefs. That, in part, has been what this book has been about.

7.40 To recapitulate the argument I have pursued here. I have argued that sense can be given to survival of death, but that survival in a miasmic or mental state is an empirical hypothesis. This seems to cut away a main ground for Poteat's distinction between 'I' and fully objective concepts. But allowing that there is something that is ineradicably existential about my situation, such that we are driven to use mythic language, the myth of the Last Judgment or of the Resurrection of the Body remains merely a picture unless it is connected up to relationship with an independently existing God. But questions about the existence of such a Being arise, so that it is wrong to suppose with Poteat and Wittgenstein that there are no reasons for preferring one picture to another, one eschatology to another. There are reasons for not believing in a retributive hell: and it would be important, if one denied such a belief, that folk were not given the impression, through the use of eschatological images, that they might have to face torture after death. This is one case where it makes an important difference as to how 'realistically' the pictures are taken. It is not enough to say in such cases that a 'realistic' belief in survival is superstition; for the criteria of what count as superstitions are heavily involved in the criteria of truth in religion. For this and other reasons the implicit irrationalism of the Wittgensteinian approach is to be rejected. As for types of survival: miasmic or mental survival is an empirical possibility, but is not much relevant to religion, though it would be of profound importance, if established, to the biological sciences. Such survival does not fundamentally alter the framework within which religious belief operates. It might be possible to make sense of recreation (or resurrection) in heaven, given that one can make sense of the concept of God (and of fellowship with him). But whether it involves some contradiction (e.g. in relation to personal identity) is obscure: so that it is best to be agnostic as to whether anything real corresponds to this picture of a consummation at the end of history. Hope of such a state is not ruled out. But the main ground for belief in it, namely the present attainment of the peace of God, renders the hope less significant. For gaining the peace of God is already overcoming death. One might say: the more the faith, the less the hope – or, if you like, those who wish to cling to future bliss themselves betray a lack of participation in eternal life.

POSTSCRIPT

WE have tried to think our way through a number of the central issues raised by the claims of religion to give a true account of the world in which we live. No doubt the solutions offered to the problems are not satisfactory; and there are other problems besides these. But at least the attempt to find solutions represents part of the enterprise of thinking about religion and about the nature of man. It is this enterprise which is important, and if this book can do anything to stimulate it, it will be sufficiently justified. But beyond the thinking about living, there is living.

SOME SUGGESTIONS FOR FURTHER READING

Articles in journals are not mentioned here, as most readers do not have access to them, but some of the references are to articles collected in book form. The numbers on the left refer to the paragraphs of the text, e.g. 1.11 refers to the eleventh paragraph of the first chapter.

Abbreviations Used

NEPT   A. Flew and A. MacIntyre (editors), *New Essays in Philosophical Theology*, SCM Press, London, and Macmillan, New York.

HSPR   N. Smart (editor), *Historical Selections in the Philosophy of Religion*, SCM Press, London, and Harper and Row, New York.

AIPA   J. Hospers, *An Introduction to Philosophical Analysis*, Routledge and Kegan Paul, London.

LL (1) and LL (2)   A. Flew (editor), *Logic and Language*, First and Second Series, Basil Blackwell, Oxford.

1.11 HSPR, ch. 1 (Plato); ch. 15 (Hegel); ch. 18 (Kierkegaard).
1.12 HSPR, ch. 19 (Mansel); ch. 5 (Aquinas).

2.1 & following HSPR, ch. 13B.
2.2 John Baillie, *The Idea of Revelation in Recent Thought*.
2.9 N. Kemp Smith, *The Philosophy of David Hume*, ch. 14.
2.11 LL (1), ch. 4; LL (2), ch. 2.

2.14 AIPA, chs, 1 & 2; A. J. Ayer, *The Problem of Knowledge*, ch. 2, ii.
2.23 AIPA, ch. 3, ii.
2.24 AIPA, ch. 4, pp. 234ff.
2.25 NEPT, ch. 3, p. 37.
2.34 LL (2), ch. 6.
2.36 NEPT, ch. 14, pp. 257f.
2.37 NEPT, ch. 13, iv.
2.39 NEPT, ch. 14.
2.41 A. J. Ayer, *The Problem of Knowledge*, ch. 3, iv.

2.48 A. R. Vidler (editor), *Objections to Christian Belief.* pp. 57f.
2.49 NEPT, ch. 12; J. Robinson, *Honest to God.*

3.2 HSPR, ch. 14.
3.3 S. Körner, *Kant*, ch. 5, iii.
3.5 S. Körner, *Kant*, ch. 7.
3.9 E. H. Hutten, *The Language of Modern Physics*, ch. 5, iv.
3.10 AIPA, ch. 4, iii; S. Körner, *Kant*, ch. 7.
3.14 NEPT, ch. 8.
3.15 P. Nowell-Smith, *Ethics*, ch. 20.
3.16 S. Körner, *Kant*, pp. 155f.
3.19 AIPA, ch. 4, iii.
3.25 AIPA, pp. 320ff.; R. J. Hirst, *Problems of Perception.*
3.35 S. Körner, *Kant*, pp. 91ff.
3.55 D. Roberts, *Existentialism and Religious Belief*, ch. 5.
3.59 S. Körner, *Kant*, chs. 1 & 2.

4.1 HSPR, ch. 5.
4.3 NEPT, ch. 3.
4.4 HSPR, ch. 4.
4.5 HSPR, pp. 63ff.; pp. 251ff.
4.8 LL (2), ch. 5.
4.10 HSPR, pp. 67ff.
4.13 HSPR, ch. 14; NEPT, ch. 3.
4.19 A. J. Ayer, *Language, Truth and Logic*, 2nd edn.
4.20 H. Bondi & others, *Rival Theories of Cosmology.*
4.27 HSPR, ch. 8.
4.37 HSPR, ch. 14B.
4.38 HSPR, p. 70.
4.39 NEPT, pp. 42f.
4.41 HSPR, ch. 13A.
4.45 HSPR, pp. 260ff.
4.55 HSPR, p. 267.
4.56 HSPR, p. 69.
4.60 Alan Montefiore, *A Modern Introduction to Moral Philosophy*, p. 43 & ch. 4.
4.70 A. R. Vidler (editor), *Soundings*, ch. 5.

5.1 HSPR, ch. 22.
5.5 NEPT, ch. 7.
5.8 N. Smart, *Reasons and Faiths*, ch. 2.
5.9 W. T. Stace, *Mysticism and Philosophy*, ch. 1, iv.
5.10 N. Smart, *A Dialogue of Religions.*
5.17 HSPR, pp. 423ff.
5.24 S. Freud, *The Future of an Illusion; Moses and Monotheism.*
5.38 W. T. Stace, *Mysticism and Philosophy*, ch. 5.
5.49 A. R. Vidler (editor), *Soundings*, ch. 5.

6.1 HSPR, ch. 24.
6.2 NEPT, ch. 6, i.
6.3 NEPT, ch. 8.
6.4 HSPR, p. 465.
6.5 HSPR, p. 152.
6.9 N. P. Williams, *The Ideas of the Fall and of Original Sin.*
6.11 NEPT, ch. 8.
6.14 HSPR, p. 471.
6.29 HSPR, ch. 10B.
6.31 NEPT, ch. 6, i.
6.37 HSPR, p. 452.
6.47 S. I. Benn and R. S. Peters, *Social Principles and the Democratic State*, ch. 8.
6.50 HSPR, p. 486.

7.2 L. Wittgenstein, *Tractatus Logico-Philosophicus*, tr. D. F. Pears and B. M. McGuinness.
7.3 W. D. Hudson, *Ludwig Wittgenstein, the bearing of his philosophy upon religious belief*, ch. 5.

7.4 Wittgenstein, *Tractatus*, 3.11.
7.5 *ibid.*, 6.431, 6.4311.
7.6 D. Z. Phillips (editor), *Religion and Understanding*, p. 127 & p. 199.
7.13 P. F. Strawson, *Individuals*, ch. 6.
7.16 D. Z. Phillips (editor), *Religion and Understanding*, p. 208.

7.23 L. Wittgenstein, *Lectures and Conversations on Aesthetics, Psychology and Religious Belief*, ed. Cyril Barrett, pp. 53ff.
7.24 *ibid.*, p. 71.
7.37 *ibid.*, p. 56.

INDEX

The numbers in the Index refer to paragraphs of the text